Massachusetts's Best Emerging Poets

An Anthology

Compiled and Edited by
Z Publishing House

2017

Table of Contents

Foreword, or How This Series Came to Be

There is a troubling catch-22 that exists in the world of publishing: in order to be published—at least by any of the major houses—you must already have been published. The logic works like this: Publishing houses want to sell books. What easier way to sell books than by publishing authors who already have amassed large followings of readers to whom they can market? Inevitably, this cycle leaves the aspiring author with the pressing question of where to begin. Sure, the dramatic rise of self-publishing platforms has enabled everyone to put their writing out there, which is great, but it does come with its own set of problems. Namely, when everyone actually does put their writing out there, as has happened, the question now becomes: Where are the readers to begin? With the oversaturation of the market, readers could spend entire lifetimes buying and reading self-published books and still not find that one author with whom they truly resonate. On Amazon alone, for instance, a new book is uploaded every five minutes, and that number is only set to rise as more and more people take advantage of the self-empowering platforms available to writers today.

The good news is that readers want to discover new talent. This we learned firsthand after beginning Z Publishing in November of 2015. What started as a small Facebook group designed to bring independent writers together on a shared platform of exposure soon transcended into a wave of newfound appreciation for independent writing. Within a few short months, Z Publishing had amassed tens of thousands of followers across social media. Once we knew the idea had struck a chord with a growing group of people, we took the next step and launched Z Publishing's own website in March of 2016. Publishing articles from writers of a multitude of genres—including travel, fiction, politics, lifestyle, and, of course, poetry—the website garnished more support from readers and writers alike, and our following continued to grow.

Though writers of several genres contributed greatly in the early months following Z Publishing's launch, the tremendous support from the poets in particular convinced us that Z Publishing's mission was an idea worth pursuing. We began to receive hundreds of submissions from poets across social media. Many of whom thanked us personally for the extra exposure. In fact, we should have been thanking them, the creators of the great content that had brought the readers to Z Publishing in the first place. Regardless, the poets displayed a level of support for Z Publishing that we never could have expected, and so when we decided it was time to take the next step in Z Publishing's evolution and publish our first official book, we knew exactly who to turn to.

Even though we had high expectations, the result of Z Publishing's first book publishing attempt was truly surprising: Fifty talented poets, from sixteen countries, all worked with enthusiasm to produce a volume of independent poetry that could appeal to all readers of poetry, and Z Poetry: An Anthology of International Indie Poetry (Volume 1) was proudly published in August of 2016, officially marking our status as a book publisher.

Since that time, we've produced and published books in numerous genres, but we've never lost sight of our poetry roots. From state poets laureate to poets who have never before been published, we've continued to promote the work of talented wordsmiths across the globe. In our eyes, anyone who produces good content is worthy of having their work seen.

With that idea in mind, we began the America's Best Emerging Poets series, in an effort to find and promote the best up-and-coming poets on a state-by-state basis. At the end of the year, we will invite five poets from each state to contribute to a book showcasing the best emerging poets in the country, and from there, we will offer one poet our first solo book deal. To make these selections, we will rely exclusively on reader reviews, so if there are any poems within this book that you particularly enjoy, please give them a mention in your Amazon review.

Now that you know a bit about how this series came to be, we'd like to thank you for taking the time to explore the very first edition to the America's Best Emerging Poets series. We hope you enjoy this publication, and we look forward to hearing your thoughts regarding how, together, we can build the publishing house of the future.

-the Z Publishing Team

Thoughts, Reflections, and Stream of Consciousness

"I am trapped in the attic of my mind.
High above are stars that hold a spiritual power."

- Maureen DeLeo

Heavy
Roxxanna Kurtz

I can't sleep.
3 a.m. crawls into bed
next to me,
weighing down the sheets.
Its prying fingers prod
my eyes and pull me
away from tender dreams.
I lay until the earth ticks
and rolls over,
watching as streetlights
become a sun that peaks
I'm over the edge of the world,
lost in thought,
and my soul feels heavy.

A Chill
Chris Rinier

A shutter that came from someplace within
Something indescribable that makes your hair stand on skin
A flicker of realization that dissolves too swiftly to comprehend
When it transpires again, try to let it transcend

I Am Like the Night
Folasade Smith

I am like the night. Dark, mysterious, deep and profound. You come to me for clarity. You sit in my everlasting shade to become one with your thoughts. And you know what, freaks come out at night. HAHA. I love to watch them crawl from their shady posts, seeking my stars to make wishes upon and to dream and love with one another.

I am like the night. Light cannot touch me with its burning rays. I am cool and sweet, like berries in the summer. Farmers sigh with relief at the sign of my moon rising from the depths of this world. I call in the hard laborers, the animals, and the children for solitude. They look up to my moon for the man who can answer their most sacred inquiries. Who can answer their most sacred inquiries? The sun is too hot, too far to reach. The sun knows nothing of what these people wish and dream and hope for.

> I am like the night. Dark skin, cool to the touch, and sacred is my body
> which God has created
> in
> His
> image.

On Board
Hadley Heinrich

The simple duration of events is a strength in itself;   you are still here,
suspended, existing when you expected to be torn apart   by what
vaguely
intruded so long ago   a sense of your own mind in its independence
its infinite towers and trains whistling softly in their solitude   through
nights spent onboard
and the signs flashing past   and the sleeping countries   the harsh edge
of air when you reach out the window   the snap of door creak of sill screech of
brakes that continues once you jolt awake   will this inner life always be
recoiling from pain   and the fear of parting with train tracks

Impatience
Gabe Goodman

If I fail to see a transcendent narrative
spanning the life of an individual,
the causality of my
moral shortcoming involves
a dishonesty
in my own life story.
My sin stems
most often from a drunken
forgetfulness brought on by
an acute negligence,
a malnourishment of my
shame—of the spirit.

Of Martyrs and Machines
Eddie Brophy

Of martyrs and machines
And disingenuous philanthropy
Of raptures and rape
And soapbox dancing beauty queens
Of consensual deceit
And tobacco company integrity
Of farmers and pharmacies
And waiting for this cotton fever to break
Of fashion trends and Facebook friends
And a patriarchy disguised in capes and robes
The idiots always smile
But trust me, their sadness lasts all the while
Desperate for a hero, impatient for a seer
There must be another way out of here
Without suicide or crucifixion
Or through the cancer of addiction
Pornography for depression and the people it upsets
Of martyrs and machines
And the pursuit of placebo truths
The archdiocese is collecting royalties on this gold record standard
It's easier to blindly cater to pious assertions of faiths and gods
Than it is to accept there may never be any proof
Of martyrs and machines
And bibles full of ammunition
Your zealotry is an army tank
And it was your hate, not your lord that put you on this mission.

Redemption
Natasha Charest-Ciampa

Shifting my placement
running three years past my maker
glitter where my teardrops fell
used to be half but now I'm full as the moon

Brighter, stronger, stardust in my veins
and I'm the only one to thank
Forked tongues can't strike a ghost
and you're living in the past

Anecdotes of the Notes App
Wylie Thornquist

I.

One year of my life, I described the sky on the bus ride to school every morning
on my shiny new phone. In the cold of those long bus rides
       entries would read like
           jan 23, 6:58 am
              monotone overcast sky, slightly lighter where sunrise should be.
              looks but doesn't smell like rain.
In August, that middle school phone was stolen at a waterpark,
      And now I can only remember one sunrise from that long year
That morning, sometime in February
      The sky read like
          sometime after 7
          pale yellow sky over the gas station where dad sometimes stops
          bluish snow lining the trees
     the sky breaks into red on the horizon, padded by swaths of pink
And somewhere on that quiet bus, I scramble to try to catch it

II.

Vignettes illuminated by stripes of lightning
Flat grays give way to
     Layers

     And depth

In the flashes of light

     The burnt orange moon reveals itself gradually

Though dark, I see the fetal rabbit curled inside it grow

      Brighter and lighter

        As it crawls up the sky

I am on the boat immersed in the smell of salt

     With my family somewhere on the stern

     Behind me, I hear an impassioned child arguing.

In his Spiderman shirt, he points to the orange sphere on the
horizon

Surrounded by heat lightning

And insists to his older brother,

"That's not the moon; it's the moon collided with Jupiter."

I look off to the horizon

To that quietly smoldering moon rabbit
Wondering what he sees

Barbarians
Wesline Zolfonoon

We are the barbarians we feared would come
cloaked in deceit
We fooled ourselves
blinded by our wrongdoings
We never saw ourselves coming
We infiltrated the only good we had
rotting it away
We sat and waited
armed and ready
For ourselves

Maternal Instincts

Elissa Fertig

Did I ever tell you the one about your mother?
The way she dipped her eyes in the full moon
the day you were born
like cloth in dye.
She was trying to resurrect something then.
You were all water and warm plants
resting on the edge of her vision, the hair on your neck a coil of vine,
the whisper of your lashes a rocking boat.
It is important others tell you the visions of your birth,
death, the first time you walked, the first time you felt rain on your face.
You will not witness these things,
after all.

Fallen Stars
Maureen DeLeo

I am trapped in the attic of my mind.
High above are stars that hold a spiritual power,
Something which we have long since forgotten,
Long since lost our connection.
The fire crackles, suggesting life,
We need only to reach out and burn just a little.

Lullaby
Sarah Better

This is a kind of lullaby
That goes over your head
As you lay on your bed awake

And you think of her
Not of me
As you try to fall asleep
But she swims through your dreams

Like a mermaid
At sea
As I lay on the shore
With nothing to hold on to

This is your lullaby
Sleep well and sleep tight
And dream about the way
I used to look into your eyes

How do you expect me
To forget your love so easily
I know you've moved on
But I'm still stuck to memories

You were a pearl
that I found in the ocean
Come back to me
Here I'll be standing

Cause I'm yours
I want to hear your voice
Come back to the shore
And I'll sing

Your lullaby.

Honeysuckle

Greta Wilensky

All summer '17 waiting to write and
peeling dead skin off my hands.
Shiny-faced and determined
full of film reels and sweat
I drive through neighborhoods I drive
downtown my scenery its own kind of
postcard too colorful for you and you
and you. Streets jam-packed with houses
potholed roads the heat of day
and how leather clings to thighs.
The unfixed neon signs and my hand on the
steering wheel, a desire I can't crush.
Driving home close to midnight I say a prayer
and my city is preserved like this,
Khmer restaurants and liquor stores
forever. A car full of teenagers perpetually
speeding down the same state highway.
Summer brewing the same kind of love
year after year. Summer giving us so much
to sink our teeth into, so much to gnaw
off the bone. Show me your hands.
How they bend in the light. Show me
your teeth—the hopeful dog in you. I don't
pray to stay up waiting for you or anyone.
I don't pray that my city be all money and gold
foil. There's a leak in my chest and it's coming out
bubbling and bloodred. Nothing withholding.
Nobody going back. I turn around and summer
is halfway eclipsed. In this memory of my hometown
we are making out in a parked car; we are making out
behind my bedroom door. This doesn't have
to be anything you don't want it to be. Freedom is
the purest form of love. The evening sun saturating
the night in pink, money in perfect envelopes.
I love you and it's getting me nowhere. I love you and
I won't take it back. Sun lapping up the milk of my calves.
Outside, more sirens, blue lights, this again.
Everything feels like an asthma attack.
Everything feels like a four-car pileup.
So this is me, getting out of the car.
This is me, leaving the scene, walking slowly toward
the horizon, strangely backlit, standing
taller in the light.

Filter
Chris York

You drink Malbec and yell to him about the Shibuya Station crossing in Tokyo: too loud, too intimate, too popular—a cocktail for comfort for all those involved. I'm rooted in the corner, clumsily trying to grow into the wall.

My friend finds me, somehow, and begins to tell me about a Catalonian-looking girl in oversized glasses. *She is the personification of beauty! She is Beauty! I wonder if those glasses are prescribed? You should talk to her! I should talk to her!*

I nod, not wanting to miss a wink, a touch, the way your eyes scream like neon signs to bored country folk. KARAOKE! LIVE MUSIC! FULL NUDITY! You laugh and the eight-legged monster comes to life—flesh from metal, blood from desire, wine from water—ruining the Gaijins' photo op. I run around the mountain of cars and find myself lost in the Imperial Palace

again. *Which way to the Pakistani embassy? Don'ttouchmymoustache.*

No—that's wrong. But hey, I can use chopsticks and slurp audibly now. I stop when I hear Buddha weeping; you buy knickknacks at his retreat and carry them into his oxidized belly. Your mother is inebriated, cursing your friends: they're thoughtless! Careless! Wait—I hope you enjoyed the cheese spread. My hands are drenched as your father rummages around in your backpack while you sprint around the train station looking for the ticket in the front pocket. I walk out and join the crowd.

Trimming my Trees
Mara Donofrio

The deeper I hike into my field, the less I can talk about yours, or anything really
Besides what happens between "What hurts?" and "Come back if it still hurts"
I think we should talk—can you relate your java code to a cardiac code?
I'd like to use my words, but these are the only ones I have left
The others are shy veins that duck from searching needles
They're hiding when I need them and my sentences refuse to bleed
My prefixes and suffixes are all -itis and -osis—not even spellcheck catches my drift
My synapses are being clipped like Pangaea is splitting and everyone jumped to
one continent
It's hard to see the trees when the whole forest is burning

Holding Grudges
Christina Mondy

I like to hold grudges

I gingerly pick them up
All red hot and pulsing
I place them on the counter
Dust them off until they shine
I wipe the goo out of their eyes
Wrap them in a wool blanket
I almost give them a bath
But they would rather rest

I hold them by my chest
Softly stroke their heads
I kiss the tips of their noses
And hum a gentle song
I keep them fed and watered
So they grow and thrive
I will always keep them with me
And we will grow old and happy

My grudges and I, forever.

Insomnia
Kimberly Dacorogna

As I reluctantly close
my windows to the world,
out of the darkness
comes my bully.

Grim, troubled being
in need of company,
she visits every night,
taunts me with visions
of missed opportunities:

« Il était juste là. Tu aurais pu parler. »

I slam my eyes tight,
count my breaths
in an attempt
to shut her out.
I writhe out of her tight grip
Nearly.

She retaliates, strikes
me harder this time
with regrets, and recollections
of words uttered
out of anger:

« Je n'ai pas envie de te parler,
je te déteste! »

I gasp, reach for
air, my breath
stuck somewhere
between my lungs
and my lips.

I'm in dire need of
relief, but insomnia
has outlawed sleep
by her edict.

Deforestation

Traci "Troi Justice" Williams

I am tasteless fruit
fallen from broken limbs
of generations of decaying trees
broken men and women

chasing forbidden fruit
cross-pollinating
affixing themselves
to other broken women and men

in a search to become whole
Heart rot
at the center of the ancestral trunk
difficult to prevent

Each ring a concentric circle
dating the competition
the natural reaction to grow towards the light
a continuous growth-wound of the sacrifice

that was not and will not be
Not one elder willing to bend away from the sun
so, the younger can grow upwards
closer to The Son

Diseased heartwood, weakness, and breakage
prevalent throughout the family forest
Hardwoods complacent
Seedlings falling over

Friday, Three O'clock
H.M Zahra

As the seconds brake, honk, and clutter end to end,
Packed like processed fish and
Going nowhere in a rush;

As I sit in my gliding chair, inert save
Clacking fingers and eyes
Scanning past ordered vacuums,
I imagine myself running: my lungs are new
And my legs like machines—
I don't know where I'm going.

I don't flee towards home; my house is flat, empty.
I live like I work:
With lukewarm efficiency.

I don't boil, I simmer slow. No wasted effort. When I go,
I won't explode from pressure,
But deflate like old dreams.

My seat is cushioned soft, my boss artless and mild;
He walks in with a smile
And leaves unchanged completely.

Pleasant, sure, but static. Workers cased in amber
Are babbling as they amble.
I sit and watch and wait.

I don't know what I'm waiting for. It seems I exist
In the negative spaces
Of Fate. Forgotten, perhaps.

Or ignored. My thoughts collapse—four o'clock chimes.
Existential crises
Are good to pass the time.

The Storyteller
M. P. Mason

The storyteller is not as open
as the books she writes
nor the elegant poetry
leaping from her fingers.
The words on the page
are her savior,
her protector,
her white knight.
For in writing she can express
what her mouth refuses to.
And in these stories,
behind which she hides,
the truth is easy to deny.
For though she loves her manuscripts
and the beauty they supply,
her walls are made of iron-gray,
through which only pages can escape.

She and I
Erica Gilman

She tapped at my window last night. The night was hazy, stuffy with undone things and
responsibilities. It was intoxicating and my lungs drown in the thick of it. I unlocked the
window, pulled the dirty glass up, and peeked out suspiciously. After peering around in the dark
air, I saw her back moving away from the light of the moon.

She glanced at me and then continued on her way into the woods.

For a moment, I thought about going back to bed, I was so tired. Sleeping felt so natural, I slept
throughout the day and night out of necessity. But instead, I put leg after leg, head after feet,
until I stumbled into the damp grass that curled under the pads of my feet.

I followed her trail.

Trudging through the woods, without a glimpse of her, I was almost ready to give up. When I
finally made it to the clearing, there was the lake, the lake I grew up on. And there she was,
standing on the other end of the reflecting pool. There was a breeze, and for a moment the air
loosened its grip around my neck. I could breathe, and she felt closer to me. Everything was alive
as I looked at her. I remembered it all.

We breathed in the fresh air, then turning, I took us back home.

1861-2017
Michael Anthony

Rain and wind pluck dead leaves
Finally gone after months, years
Creaking
As if on rusted hinges and being meticulously loosened, routinely
Built during the civil war. A stop along the Underground Railroad
Certainly
You can tell by the red window near the servant's stairs
Stained, like Margaret after her habitual bottle of Pinot
Addictive is an adjective, in English
Addicting is a present participle, in Massachusetts

wisdom searcher
Iris Lapaix

my soul is a wanderer searching for
why's—
the artifacts
and memories within the between.
Peeling the surface
for an understanding of between the line.

Wearing comfort in my irises so that
Trust
eventually, mentally, and emotionally
decide to join us.
Allowing myths, rumors, stories,
and experiences intertwined with history
to wander into the vibrators of my
eardrums to open la paix of what
really truly is within each peripheral.

Life & Memories

"Memories of the mind drift along the river of life,
Memories that were just—memories.
The heart is pure but His mind decays
dissolving like rocks on a shore."

- H.B. Harris

Hands
Gaia DeNisi

We are born, fingers outstretched.
Reaching towards the world.
Hands
Open and empty.
Holding nothing
Anticipating everything
And ready to hold on.
Tight.

Hands that press on the soft carpet
Fingers entangling in its loose fibers.
Pulling the body forward.

Fists encircling the smoothness of their first crayon
Pressing it against the infinity of whiteness.

Hands that grip the round metal
Dangling above the wood chips of the playground.
Cold biting into fingers
Which refuse to let go.
Rosy from the cold, they return home.
Triumphant.

Hands that shoot into the air
Fueled by excitement.
Hands that society has not yet taught
How unacceptable it is to care.

Hands that turn pages
That catch and throw.
Hands that make daisy chains
And pick blackberries.
Blackberries so full of life
Bursting.
The dark juice staining pricked fingers.
Hands.

Hands that laugh and hands that cry
That gently wipe a tear from someone's cheek
Encircling their sobbing body
And holding them.
Tight.

Hands reaching for the warmth of another.
Fingers entangling with theirs.

Hands.
Wrinkled and worn.
Bent with age and memories.

Holding everything.
Anticipating nothing.
Hands.

Derelict
Madeline Gilmore

Often, I walk this road
and come to what I think I can avoid:
the old house on stilts,
white as the snow around it,
the salt-strewn path,
hollow as the birdsong in the eaves,
the little that we leave
behind—and when I go,
the black door burning my eyes,
the knob that once was golden.

History in the Isle
K. Dawn Liu

your face   a mirror
through which i look to see
through the haze
and i see my own,
peeled of years and scars—
a naked
plucked passenger pigeon.

a surge of flooding
and waves push me as i
watch your face,
the empty space
in my body
heaving with indifference

and soon i am an island,
bald and brown with porcupine shrubs,
watching you, watching
the waves as they
rise and lap at the heart of me.

fog, fog undo, fog again.
we are the dirt of this lump;
the wave is in me and i try
to keep us in steady sight

but then what is it—
i am rinsed out to sea by the passing.

White Lines
Davina Daines

You used to tell me
The scars would fade
So my first night in the ward
When the nurse wasn't looking
I unbent a paperclip
And carved a smile with it

I felt invincible

Like that night in August
I came home from the unit
For the first time since March
I was wearing a black sweater two sizes too big
It was eighty-two degrees

When I opened the door
Finn came running with his new Lego set
Dad grabbed champagne
I was limbless when Mom let go

We cooked together
In our ovenless kitchen
String beans popping in the pan
Chilean seabass browned in butter

When I handed Mom the plates
My sleeves fell to my elbows
And I knew she knew, then
I knew she knew

Wrists tattooed with white lines
Crisscrossed like pick-up sticks
And raised
Like pumped-up veins on T

I loved her more then
Than I ever thought I could
Her tears
Sharper than any wire
I bent

Do Not Look to Pass, Go
Laura Cafasso

A glimmer:
a family rearranged to START
before the whammies, the wins, the wisdom.

Before fate rejected our cards and said GO FISH.

It throbs like Gatsby's Green Light
across any horizon I find myself on. A memory.
The lightest lightness I ever felt.

I was a mermaid
flickering between the shallow and the deep
recoiling at regurgitated leaves and bugs stuck in the pool filter.

Sleek scales made me lightning, a torpedo
able to race insatiable sharks, avoid plastic anemones
and churn whirlpools.

Baited, we'd go limp in the current
riding foam seahorses, gazing at the summer sunset.

Had I known that moment would burn out,
maybe I wouldn't have slipped into my sea legs.

A distant, chlorine-tinged memory—
lost like sea turtle carcasses in the aquarium.
I rarely dive to retrieve it; it's too painful.

I let it dangle in my periphery,
glittering like salt sunbaked into beach rocks.
Intangible because tangible things break.
A constant image of yesterday, when we just passed GO.

Life in Screens
Mick Theebs

I'm paid to stare at a screen
And after a long day of staring at screens
I can think of no better way
To cut loose and find reprieve
Than going home and staring at screens.
And when it comes time
To go to sleep
I lay my head
And close my eyes
And stare at dreams
On the screen
Of my mind.

Eight Months
Victoria Pulvidente

moonlight wraps around her bare shoulders
hands rest gently on her pregnant belly
she stares out the window
the drapes create shadows as they sway
her husband lays silently in bed
with the white sheets pulled under his chin
fresh stubble forms a crescent
little puffs of breath flee from his mouth
she hums quietly to herself
a lullaby for the baby
about the moon and the sea
her face scrunches
freckles pinch together
as the baby tenderly kicks
her lips slightly part
eyes soften and she continues to hum

Human?

Kiana Govoni

Dirt everywhere,
and I watched them eat
at the special dining table.

This is not always true;

The pack let me sit with them sometimes—
the sounds not always animal
or human,

It wasn't the worst.

There's this safety in the dark some fear—
I hide there, I do,
but not always, for I'm human, too.

At least I think I still am, and I need touch, too.

The pack dines at night and when I can
I bare my teeth like them in crazy,
slapping hands, and I believe them.

Yes, this is mine.

Disease pollutes the air all day,
streets laughing at the wicked ones,
and me, of course, at me.

People who look or act like me—

They say that I'm the omega,
so used to the bottom
that I welcome it.

Even when there's time to run away, I don't.

I didn't run into the wild
or fall into an endless hole;
I could have become a better me.

But truthfully, I didn't.

greenhouse poem
Kyle Calise

i used to work in a greenhouse
it was so hot
and the days passed by like so many flowers

i used to work in a greenhouse
i would fill my water bottle three times a day
—for drinking and rinsing my arms—

one day i cut off the bottoms of my jeans
to make shorts in the summer heat

one day i cut off my insecurities
in a green sea of belonging

Eric on a motorcycle at a stop light
Aidan Meyer-Golden

All of the poets in my life are crazies
—perfectors of speech idiosyncratic and stirring to the gut.
I listen and emulate, gulp their babble.
All of the crazies in my life are poets
—enough distant to imbue a clenched palm with an essence
a less-considered materialism would reject.
Emulating these crazies my hands seem to constantly be giving me away
in places I try to dissemble.
Suddenly they'll visit me in a dream
and recite a few verses, standing there awkwardly,
and I wake wanting to be honest as a bell, or morning ravens.

Warm Coffee
Anapurl Feldman

Heaven is a diner
is a green booth in the corner
by the dust-screened window
is sitting across from you,
as my feet leave footprints
from your sandy eyes
to the tower of empty creamers
our fingers did not have the agility
to scale.

If you sit on the right side,
everyone is happy.
One waitress is all cheeky smiles
and sarcastic quips, while the other is all
dark half circles and black make up,
rough canine teeth and unsavory gum.

We met a magician,
he was quite impressive
with his shirt buttons lopsided and his words a little sideways,
he tricked us with an ace
left his number on the inside.
I laughed, you glared.

The coffee is the kind of watered down
that tastes so good at 3 AM,
each refill a new wave of conversation,
crashing against our ankles,
slowly washing away the trail of earth and dirt,
I carried from your eyes.

I have no proof they were here before
you mentioned them, sand grains rubbed into my face,
below my eyes, across my nose,
brown tattoos to remind me of you.

When the glow of 4 AM
beckons us outside, and Heaven transforms
from a place of the drunk and the fallen
into just another diner, lights buzzing off
with the onset of dawn—

I will tell myself these freckles are here
for camouflage, to help me hide beneath
dark coffee and murky water,
because I kind of like it
when seaweed sticks to my feet.

Heaven is a diner
full of animated voices, laughter
and the sound of dishes clumsily kissing countertop
on purple, hot, heavy, breath-held summer nights,
with over buttered toast and runny eggs,
a stolen moment for nostalgia's sake.

My hot chocolate got cold,
and I didn't realize it was drizzling,
until I saw the streaks like bullets
fracturing the glow of orange streetlights,
on the way back to your house full of muses,
tapestries, and silhouettes.

Your bed was an island, where we went
when Heaven's open sign flickered off,
once all the angels slept off their otherworldly glimmer,
put on their human masks the next day.

It was heaven because it did not last.

Antiquated Marvel
N.F.H.M.

We begin
Underneath
Overshadowed
By dusk
That stenches
Salty grains of sand

Forbidden
They say
To marvel
From this viewpoint
Eroded by dunes
A bleached lantern; blinding moon

One score
And ten
We have thus
Begun

Purest
Visibility
Antiquated
Compassion

Darkness

Tim DiFazio

my eyes squeezed shut,
the damage nearly undone
     i see that darkness is not
          a blanket (ice-cold) meant to shut out the world
          a straitjacket (too loose) to protect me from myself
          a shield (of air) to crouch behind until i disappear—
    no, not a prison;

the night expands infinitely outward:
an endless canvas for the mind to fill.

In His Mind
H.B. Harris

Memories of the mind drift along the river of life,
Memories that were just—memories.
The heart is pure but His mind decays
dissolving like rocks on a shore.
The remnants of the past washing away,
Away they wash from His life.
At night, his footsteps echo through the darkness,
Searching for the light in His blindness.
No light is found but sounds are heard,
Sounds of the faucet that
drip,
drip,
and drip.
Time is but an enemy,
Ticks eating at His serenity.

Entry from Skybox Imaging
Lev Craig

At night I look through foreign journals for your name.
The painted cinderblocks cold against my shoulderblades
when I lean against the wall flies sleeping
and I taste the water in my mouth. Already the dogs
are forcing themselves up through the hyperlinked forest
and the woman who leads the goats arrives. A dark red string. A rifle
given like bread. Bread given like bread. A knife
in the garden like fruit. This is fruit: shaving cream
half-empty on the kitchen sink; sand congealing
in the drain; dark hair on my legs; thickly matted
animal; the burrs at the top of the dunes; my knuckles
in the morning; who can know when things like this
will happen. I bite my lips instead of yours.

Kristallnacht
Dana Shahar

this is not white smoke
i am breathing out my nostrils.
this is not blood crusting my fingernails.

it is not glass or metal;
there are no little shards of broken windows.

i did not run away or
change my name in order to
save the skin
on my bones
by hiding in a grime-slathered closet
for three years
so that one day,
ten years later,
i could raise a healthy family.

the sky was not ashen,
nor orange, nor blue.
there were no clouds.

and the slow, slimy steps I took
were not sloshing mud
or crushing pieces of Jewish perseverance.

the stars fell from the sky that day
and lined the streets.

A Revolution in Mourning
Ashley Puddester

I spent a year isolated and yearning
Betrayed that without you, the planet kept turning
I abstained from this world, frozen in time
Helplessly reliving a scene of no crime
So long ago, you shielded me
From a sight much like what I would see
A morbid view of my fallen creator
The corpse awaits all of us, sooner or later
Three hundred sixty-five, in a landfill of grief
Four seasons later, I get a glimpse of relief
A light in the darkness from my trip around the sun
My future is still coming, but for you there is none.

Motherhood
Jordana Joy

I squat, a wind of
June, or the end
Of May, nestled in the thrill
Of sunken, mellow dirt
Upon my crest of my knee.

The air rummages, crisp against
The ears of the town. Someone,
Listening, picks up a shovel.
The hacking of long days
Pile upon the sun, the daybreak.

Upside-down, a baby,
Held by heels, conscious
To the head-toe impact of
Burping. It is primal and distinct.
We talk in these old ways.

New in the most antiquated of ways,
Struggling in the shininess of a flat cap
Or the perusing of a dusty black shoe,
The way that discovery rears a head or
Two; in a freakish, abhorred glare.

The stop and go flow of grains, beaded
With seeds upon their heads, tossed
In and around and about, the way that
We do. And, with a shuffle, the dirt upon my knee

Is dispersed.

They Always Said I Had a Great Imagination, and Probably Depression or Something

Megan Alyson Barnes

I close my eyes and I see myself running naked
Diving through holes covered in brush
Leaping over hills and across state lines
I open my eyes and I'm still in my bed
An hour later and I'm still in my bed
Two days later and I'm in my bed but I don't know if I'm *still* in my bed

I try to keep my eyes open as much as I can
As I submerge myself under the water coming from my shower head
My eyes sting but they're open and I'm here in this world
But they close by obligation and there's this old woman behind me again
She hates my vitality and has melted skin, she moves her body toward mine
And her hand reaches my abdomen
I force my eyes open using my fingers as artillery and defense
Burning, but getting through the pain
I can't believe I have to do this just to survive another Tuesday morning
I mean, Thursday morning
Did I wash my hair?

I look into the mirror and down at the counter
Then down at the floor and now I'm on the floor
Tracing the grooves between the tiles
Seeing the small squares form bigger squares
Until the whole bathroom is one big square
Now I see the whole house is just one big square
So is the neighborhood and so is the town
The geometrics extend outwardly
And I can see why someone could think the world is flat
I can also see that I need to clean this disgusting bathroom again

I see myself running
Running away from the succubae and squares
And at this point, I don't know if my eyes are open or closed
For once I just want to run for something
And I want to make it past the frame of my bed

Gum

Julia V. Pretsfelder

Play-Doh's kinsman
of the chemically inflated name
molds along the palette
only for mangling more,
for wrestling meaningless
and innocent battles
in the grips of the tiniest jaw
to make limp,
insipid, and overwrought
by the then-tired tongue;
to feel a pop of pride
while manipulating sapped
strips to surging bubbles
through unasthmatic wheezes
whose perky pink
bouncy-house walls deflate
like clumsily handled footballs
resuscitated by pensive, wavering sighs,
meticulously sculpted, thinned balloons,
become over-capacitated and snapped
by rambles and caustic curses,
cooler than the mint flavor
but much less fleeting,
as rebellious ruptures repeat
with malleable finesse
until there is no song or suspicion
to exhale into fragile confines.

Family & Friends

"My lovely lifegiver,
one half of this conspiracy we call heritage
I see the way your parts match my parts."

- Charlotte Koch

From the Ship to the Lighthouse
Katherine Nazzaro

Listen,
I have meant freedom,
        meant solitude,
                meant isolation.
Boards shrunk from a stinging spray—
I have been out here too long.
I have been tossed around like a child's bath toy.
The sea has always been coldly apathetic,
        but winter storms have made it frigid.

I have been out here for too long.

You are not a harbor,
        there is no welcome here.
No hot drink for comfort,
        no rest to speak of.
A beam cuts through fog the way a siren
pierces a silent night.
        Remind me again that I'm almost home.

The rocks are sharp, the sea is cold,
        but you are still there.
The waves grow taller,
until they're the whole world,
and you're still there.
Turn off the lights,
        but you're still there.
Change the paint,
        but you're still there.

I will go back to the sea
        and sail the world again.
I will be tossed by the waves
                —again.
Even in harbor, even anchored down,
I am built for movement.
You, my love, remain
and remind me I'm almost home.

The sea is cold, the rocks are sharp,
but it's all ending soon.

Missing
Lizz Wilson

Losing someone as child
leaves you with pictures that you hate,
all seemingly from your awkward, fat stage.
With questions you can't answer
that strangers are always asking.
With apologies you don't want
accompanied by similar stories,
you didn't ask to hear.
With an empty stocking at Christmas time
that you don't want to throw away,
nor designate as the new dog's.
To fill with squeaky toys and bones.
With old sweatshirts
that have lost their familiar smell.
With an old lighter
decorated with a pinup girl;
her bra falls when you ignite the flame.
With a little brother you never see
because your parent in common is gone,
his other doesn't bother
to meet you halfway.
With an uncle,
now an only child.
Taking all the kids to Disney
to make up for the pain.
With faded memories,
unsure if they happened,
or a combination of what you've gathered
from others along the way.

Trace the Lines
Jake Phillips

On my back like you used to—

like when we were eleven,
and I took you on our first date,
where we ate cheese pizza in a private booth
then went to your mom's apartment
and snuck onto your brother's musty bed;

like when we were fourteen,
and my dad drove us around
in his maroon Toyota,
and I would watch amber streetlight
flash across your face
before we whisked into darkness again;

like when we were seventeen
and drew a crime scene
from our collapsed bodies
in chalk on your driveway,
then walked through the woods
and slow danced on a construction site
until our phones died and the moon fell from the sky;

like when we were twenty,
and I joined you and your cigarette
to break weeks of silence,
to remember the way you smiled
when you weren't high,
to remind you that thinking of me
only when you stargaze
isn't quite enough.

Geography Lessons
Alec Suthy

i walk alongside you in silence
or is it the other way around
which of us follows the other
these days

at first, you were the continent, and i
a small and steadfast island in the archipelago of your offspring

but now i desire more
and having grown
our tectonic plates collide
causing mountains of sorrows between us
but moving us closer yet

we thought these ridges drove us apart
but in some way they connect us
each trite argument a small story later
after an admittance of sorrow from your mouth or mine

i know we are not equal
you a plateau of strength
and i the valley of ashen flower
but we rely on one another
two hemispheres set upon each other
a planet and its moon

Pater

Charlotte Koch

I sense your close protective patriarch,
my proof of your paternity,
not through your recognition—
but the short puffs of breath we push from our lungs
simultaneously, pulling us through the woods
one unit moving in time.

My lovely lifegiver,
one half of this conspiracy we call heritage
I see the way your parts match my parts.
My profile resembles yours in ways I never much wanted
and yet rely on pathologically, that define the machine
that runs this body.

Our steps mirror perfectly the precise time we place our feet
on the ground, how we talk and sometimes *really* talk
but it's purely about the rhythm of our pace
of our hearts, pulsing together,
protecting us from the all too similar thoughts
that prey in these woods.

BFFs
Christine Evers

She was popular
And had her own bathroom.
We dressed up like pop stars
And ran up and down the stairs.
She moved away.
Far away.

She had a sweatshirt with a monkey on it
And she was very tall.
I never saw her cry.
But, then again, she never really laughed.
She changed.
I didn't.

She had a gap between her front teeth
And her mom taught me how to knit.
We made a fort in her closet
And did our science homework.
She moved away too.
Far away.

I didn't like her at first.
She wore frilly socks with crocs
And her cats were cute.
But, her family kind of creeped me out.
So, I stopped coming.

He had a funny name
And knew how to solve a Rubik's cube.
He had scars on both his elbows
And he taught me how to play blackjack.
Last I heard he was in Morocco.

She always smelled of lavender
And she had stubby little fingers.
She wore a cross
And loved mac and cheese with pepper.
I thought I knew her.
I guess I didn't.

Reduced to Receipts
Nicole Cerundolo

Our friendship started smoothly:
days of planning road trips on star charts,
swapping smiles and secrets like currency,
a harmony of chords from different keys

We were each other's complement,
juggling scrapbooks of inside jokes,
remarking on the beauty neither one of us could see
when we looked in the mirror

I can't pinpoint where we fell out of step,
when you shoved splinters under my nails
and built bridges out of balsa wood
just to burn them down again

You tell me I've changed—
I ask you how easy it is to keep a heart soft
after piecing it together seven times,
or seventy-seven

My limbs are weighed down
by Duco cement
but the glue hasn't dried yet;
and your words stick to the cracks

I don't think I can say goodbye
when I still want to undo our hello

Little brother

Anna Johnson

Little brother, certain nights disrobe in
the dark, rise as ripples, spreading,
settle: nights of shivering candles, of
racing down the stairs in our Sunday
clothes (dark velvet jumper, the ever-
erecting collar), stumbling in stocking
feet. Nights of M&M's in vanilla ice
cream, blue tongue to match your
Dodgers   little   league   uniform,
oversized plastic spoons appearing in
the silverware drawer in vain hope of
passing   for   metal,   vanishing
mysterious as mist.

And speaking of *m*, of the mouth that
pushes its lips together, gently easing
their door open, remember the night
you caught me in the basement (where
we used to sit and play Zoo Tycoon)
naked with my high school boyfriend?
Later that night, the softness of Mom's
butternut squash made me squirm,
seemed a pale underbelly, when I
caught your eye the one time. I
remember HORSE and how we never
played much after, spinning around the
hoop's stand, I slipped and screamed
at the knife's pain of a violent straddle.
You started throwing the baseball too
hard, gave me bloody noses as if to
punish me for the hair that grew under
my arms, between my thighs. Our
words are no longer playing touch
football—yours beat mine hard into
the ground, shovel their mouths full of
dirt   until   they   gag   and   silence
themselves. Now

Where are you, out tonight?

I Hate That I Miss You

Nicole Boliver

I hate that I miss you
The constant tug at my heart
The pain behind my eyes
My throat closing at the smallest thing
I hate the affect you have on me
Everything reminds me of you
You sneak into my mind
Like you've sunk your claws in me
Even after I said my final goodbye
Will you ever let go?
I hate that I still go to text you
Miss being able to tell you anything
I miss having someone to talk to
No matter what time
No matter what subject
I guess I gave you too much of me
Held you on too high a pedestal
Because the moment I blocked you
It felt like you took all of me
And now I'm left to find myself
When will I be free?
When will it stop hurting?
I'm so sick of crying
Please, I'm begging
Leave me alone
I'm sick of suffering
I've had enough

Girls Who Squat
JinJin Xu

We stood behind
the big rock
& lifted our skirts
waiting to become

the boys we saw
facing walls
talking to
someone
we could not see

hand in hand
we snuck up close
peering
at taxi drivers
uncles
brothers

backs turned
they were
unrecognizable

why don't
they squat?

We ran
to the big rock
& lifted our skirts
waiting, waiting
for our bodies
to follow

Love, Romance, & Heartbreak

"In our discovery of love
we uncover hidden cracks,
step upon untouched land,
unravel tangled knots
within ourselves, in all that surrounds us, in fullness, in
togetherness."

- Zoe Barnstone-Clark

Ode to Cerulean

Shalen Lowell

There you were, on the tip of my tongue
showering me with goose-pimples
and a deep ease the shade of viridian.

Simple things untangle our complicated affections
in emotional iterations
like poetry—
murmurs of cobalt and periwinkle.

Inherited legends—lesions—
rip and rend me
as I rocket through midnight Boston on the I-93
soaked in sepia-stained nostalgia.

And yet, you're my catharsis,
my cyan-shaded coastline,
salted sea breeze.

Your warmth blankets the worn spaces of my life—
jaded porch carpet where our dog lays each night.
The fiendish light tricks me;
I see her indigo shadow, still somehow resident.

You repaired worn life-patches,
stitching up the frays
with careful strokes and kisses.

I love you
in these liminal spaces.

One More Dance
for Olivia
Will deManbey

Tell me what you're thinking of.
Tell me why you're smiling.
Whisper as the wind rolls by.
Something.
Anything.
I need to know if you feel it, too.

Another step, another turn.
Is it the rain that makes me shiver,
Or is it your eyes
Shining in the lamplight?
The touch of your hand in mine?

Too many words have gone unspoken.
Too many dances left unfinished.
Each time the impulse is bested by fear.
Feeding a longing
That grows with each touch.

I am no knight in shining armor,
Just a boy with two left feet.
Trying not to stumble.
Trying to hold you closer.
But making the same mistake
Again
And again.

It's hard to think straight
With this fluttering heart,
And that float-away feeling
That fills me up
When I hold you.

So, I wrote words on a clipboard
That I couldn't quite say.
Wrote of friends and of flowers,
Trying to let you know
What gave my world life.
Why eternity might just as well be
A patch of grass,
And your head on my shoulder.

The dance may be ending,
But it need not for long.
A hand can be offered,
A song played once more.

For I believe in magic,
In fairies,
And in us.
In a second chance at True Love's First Kiss.
And in finally finding
The perfect fit.

Bitter

Meg Maziarz

There are words that should be swallowed,
And words that should be spit out.
You taste like conflict and controversy.
You taste like denial and distrust.
Wounds are not meant to be salted,
Smite or slapped.
You remind me of lightning—
Beautiful, dangerous,
And, oh, so quick to strike.

Spring Sonnet
Eloise Lindblom

When April in her shells of morning gray
Reveals at once her swell of morning gold,
When birds expel what they've saved up to say,
Sweet luscious green the landscape slowly unfolds,
And when my bedroom window opens wide
Wind shuffling the papers on my desk,
When from awakening I cease to hide
Instead to make some toast—I must confess
Then still I love you as I did before
When days were lonely, short, severe, and pale
Some say I must in spring revere you more
As season's turning turns to fresh what's stale—
Yet your immensity transcends the days,
And my affection for you stays.

Alone
Erynne Arvisais

She's lonely at night
     but She doesn't realize it
She doesn't miss the warmth of someone else
     it's been so long, She forgot
She got used it
     to the cold bed
     to being alone
     with only the warmth and protection of the blankets

Then He came
     one night it got really late
     and He stayed over
She was surprised
     and slightly nervous
She had forgotten what it was like
     how it felt to sleep with someone else

They laid down
He immediately wrapped His arms around Her
His arms may have been long and thin
     but to Her they felt safe and warm
She curled up next to Him
     in His arms

When She put Her head on His chest
She listened to His heart
     felt it pump against Her cheek
      with every beat
She slowly realized how lonely She had been
      but with each beat
      it chipped away at Her loneliness
      the more She listened to Him
      to His heart
      to His breathing
She relaxed
      and She fell
      with each beat
      She fell a little more for Him

His smell was intoxicating
His touch was exhilarating
His eyes were mesmerizing
His smile breathtaking

He made Her excited and nervous
      yet She felt calm and safe with Him
She gets drunk off His kisses
      that morning kiss meant a lot to Her
      that would make Her day
      and She hates to admit it
      but She got addicted to His kisses
      soft and sweet
      never demanding
      always gentle
She thrives off of this kind of affection
      little touches here
      a snuggle and a kiss there
      that's all She wanted
      what She craved
His presence
His touch
Him

Note from yet Another Breakup
Ben Greenman

No, she says, that second pizza
was essential to your plan you knew
the little bear wouldn't accept
another mom so you brought it to
poison him and get him out of the way.

His Encouragement
Krish Kulka

She found this broken man, who lost his way
She didn't bother to fix him—instead, she told him she would wait
She stayed there telling him different paths to take
She showed this broken man he controls his own fate
She wanted to understand who was underneath the rubble
She wanted to understand this man's pain and struggle
She didn't judge him or make him feel ashamed
She saw the beauty in him, wondering why he was unclaimed
She didn't want him to rely on her, so she taught him how to heal
She taught him there's nothing wrong with expressing how you feel
She didn't want to become the glue that held him together
She wanted him to know he had the strength to make himself better
She watched as he gathered up all his pieces
She helped him hold the cloth has he ironed out creases
She kept him company as he failed with trial and error
She kept reminding him, a fighter doesn't give up—never
She watched his transformation and evolution into a better man
She watched his struggles from start to finish as he accomplished his plan
She will never understand fully what she did for him
She saw he was drowning and she taught him how to swim
He knows even giving her the world will fall short in comparison
He just hopes his love for him is clear and bold like a caparison.

When I Think of You
Maddie Gloo

I find you in the fragments of lake-glass on my windowsill,
worn smooth and cool, turquoise and teal
In the worn-soft crevices of a tie-dye shirt,
the scent of summer breeze down by the water

You're in my mug of warm tea, drifting loose with the tea leaves, staining my teeth
and the dentist laughs and asks if I drink a lot of caffeine—yeah, I'm constantly
sipping you

The knitted socks you got me, deliberately mismatched,
anchor me like our last embrace before departing
southbound on a dark highway

You're in the taro root ice cream, the hard-boiled eggs, the strawberry syrup
Baby shampoo, dryer sheets, radio static turned low while we chop and fry onions

I see you in the stack of flames, the itch of heat in my eyes
My fingertips trace your neat graph-paper handwriting
and I ache for you—for home

each memory of you: its own balloon

Ashley Robinson

each memory of you: its own balloon
helium-high in my hands
sometimes grasped with sweating palms

sometimes a few get loose and go
to the stratosphere,
still in eye-reach

when it's just me, it's me
and the balloons. my hands keep busy
holding them, and sometimes
I can't look away

and sometimes they're so many and so strong
one gust could send us into space forever

I make myself an anchor and with heaviness
bear down. so on the ground

it's me and the balloons

Ouroboros
Michael Baker

I'd jump into oblivion to forget your face,
the warmth of your touch,
the pressure in my chest,
how sweet your lips taste,
and the home I found in you
collapsing around me.

Crumple to a heap on the bathroom floor,
capitulating to the undertow.
No respite on the horizon.
Falling, crashing out of love.
A stabbing pain in the soul.
          Twist the knife.
Torturing myself to the tune of your face.

Drag the lake,
I won't be found.

Thousand-yard stares into nihility,
white knuckled to an idealized history
written by the beaten down and hopelessly depraved.
Praying for some semblance of inner peace.
Late night amplifies the chaos of my mind.

It's hell when I'm here.

Reset my reflexes.
Reconstruct my psyche.
The abandonment of indiscretions that die hard
and cry harder.

Driven to kill my old self so that he'll never be recovered.
Bury the parts.
Burn the thoughts.
Swish with acid.
Cleanse the palate.
Bridge the gap,
          and begin anew.

Love hard
Crash harder
And burn out the brightest.
There is no other way

Awaiting
Maura K. Flaherty

I stood in front of this crowd,
A lead suit encompassing every limb on my body,
Stretching across my chest and down to my calves.

The rope around my neck,
Some days tighter than others.
And on those days the plank was a little lower,
The gravity of my weight tightening that noose.
And as I stood tippy toed on that platform my air began to dwindle,

That same noose threatening my existence also offered a slight deceit of relief.
My hands stretched above my head,
Clenched around the rope, my knuckles whitening,
The twine burning, eating away at my palms,
But I could breathe, just a little.

And then the day came when that lead suit was finally shed,
And you would think I felt better,
And I did, but only slightly,
Because now instead of that awful, tiresome, lead suit,
I am naked.
I stand in front of this crowd, so lost, so vulnerable, so damaged.
And that noose that strangled me for the past nine months, offering me a scant
amount of support is suspended behind me,
Lurking just beyond my reach,
Swaying in the breeze, teasing me with its return.

Terrified I stand in front of it,
Awaiting its reinstatement.
I thought once finally released,
I would be free.

But I'm not,
I am weak with exhaustion,
Paralyzed by hurt,
Cemented in anger,
All strikes of a match,
Tormenting the looming fuse.

And I pray,
And I hold everything in,
Responding with "I'm good" when asked,
But I'm not.

I hate you Carlos,
I hate you so much.

Photo Diary
MaKayla M Allen

You are June, and
both views of Niagara Falls.

The disposable photos, both
when the flash did and did not
go off.

I drink you through a Wendy's straw,
and dip my finger into the foam
of you when the milk
of my latte is gone.

You were the way May would
not quit raining, despite the
Jazz I played it, or all the
times I sat in quiet resistance.

You are June, and both
the home I left
and the one I currently
am in.

Crickets
Madeleine Jackman

The saddest sound in the world
is the silence of crickets as you pass,

sauntering footsteps in a dark field
quieting the insects' crescendo,

an orchestra over surround sound
as each speaker mutes one by one,
the vacancy of an auditory experience.

Everyone wants to lay in the grass
but no one wants to do it first or alone,

under the weight of an imminent storm
the tickle of wet grass and curious ants,

regardless stay still and steady to see
the bashful fireflies flicker in time
to the hum of crickets becoming outgoing.

I'm like a cricket as he moves past me,
holding words tightly under my wings

like, I want you to love me
and I love you I love you I love you,

stay still a little bit longer so I can speak,
ask what crickets must think
in those silent spaces between chirps.

Me Remembering You
Mikayla Gordon Wexler

I fit into your arms like a sugar cube between a forefinger and thumb
over a cup of late night tea.

Your kisses were melting ice cream
on the nose of a 5-year-old, cross-legged on the town green.
They tasted like that moment right after the rain in southern Florida,
when steam rises off the tar and envelopes you from pinky toes
to last frizzy strand of hair.

I craved you,
11:59 on a December Thirty First, an end,
the sofa you sink into after a long day of listening
to caffeine melodies and tension headache rhythms.

Like bubblegum.
Expanding, stretching, familiar.
I considered attaching a piece of Trident to your back,
feel the pull of your life on my tongue.

I wanted to curl up in your corneas,
lay out in the hammock of your shoulder blades,
nestle between your eyebrows.

My blue raspberry slushy,
left me with a turned-on grin, delirious buzz.

But time never runs out of ways to close doors on fingers,
two hundred miles of silent answers to the questions leaving lonely lips,
and Saturday will always ache to kiss Friday but never find the means to turn
around.

A Road Trip Through Love
T.B. Grant

I try to search my archives, for the feelings that I'm experiencing.
I haven't been successful; this flow of energy is unknown.
These feelings feel familiar, as if I've felt them before,
But the ones of my past, can't level with the ones right here,
Right now.

I hold her hand and it's soft and gentle,
But I feel past her flesh,
And focus on her warmth, her pulse,
Her heart valleys north and south,
Her eyes, east and west.

It was a first, the ability be able to read her soul, through her eyes.
I can't figure the color, but they're light, and open.
But she wouldn't gaze into my eyes of seas,
Because she was aware, I could see, her heart as it beat.

Through organic chemistry, our bond was slowly tightening,
Not so fast, that invites spoiling,
But at a pace of naturalness, both unknown to us.
This was a synthesis of burgeoning love,
We just didn't know it yet (we did).

It's a time of season, when empty desires rot
The trees are bare of selfish wants
My crimson scattered tongues lay upon the earth,
And I only wish to live for hers,

Not a day passes where she is vibrant,
Dancing in my mind.
Her voice, full of sweet loving words,
Echo through my mind, and the burrow within my heart.

Neuroscience be damned,
This is more than timely released chemicals,
I'm in love with her in fall,
That is all. No need to ruin our splendor.

Snarky

Anika Krause

Moon out in the morning:
I assume it's a positive warning and I
greet you, brimming and toothy

I take your howareyagood
for tea leaves, reading until
the trails twist in the desired direction

I hover and hesitate, assign signs
to moons and breaths, crossing the cards
until they craft correct answers

Funny how superstition turns conviction,
even if wayfaring eyes and humble chatter
are the only evidence.

So when I burst through your door
I expected certainty, a dramatic swell
from the orchestra, the inevitable embrace

Instead, there was an empty room,
signless, and I was left aching,
staring out the window at the moonless sky.

Newton's First
Sharon Amuguni

In this reality, we stand furiously apart
believing solemnly in Newton's first
and the inability to nurture instinct out of one's seams.

I will become what grows
where all eyelids and shadows eventually combine.
The absence of light bleached into me.

You will stay too soft like rotting fruit,
fluorescent in your sickly nature.
There is no timeline in the mathematical world where we both overlap.
But, oh, pull out the numeracy latched from the teeth of the hound,
and there is potential for all things simultaneously.
There we are, fledglings of what everything could look like.

There we are Newton's first curbed into itself,
all still items reborn with flight, all winged beings plucked from the sky,
all grow hooves and horns and halos and everything belongs now as one.
The simplicity of opposition unworthy of presence,
all of this to find a moment
where neither of us said, *we're just too different,*
this love will never fully grow lungs.

Winter Heat
Amy Welch

The winter months burned
because of you.
They were warm and free
like July.

Your laugh
and my words hot off my tongue
like a child first learning to speak.
I am a fool.
A happy fool.
Happy to stay in winter just this once.

a different kind of sweet
Katrina Meserve

you have black skinny jeans with ripped holes in the knees.
if I were a bee I would inhabit those rounded spaces
to hide my honey in something sweet.
and today you dressed as a bee; I have never seen anything more loveable,
but I'm just waiting for the day our daughter first mumbles the word honey
and you'll have been beaten.
I would call you the bee's knees and hope that
brought a smile to your face as the wind tickled your leg's
exposed midriff.
imagine our daughter in a bee costume among a field of
wildflowers.
ten seconds, think about it,
please tell me you're smiling.
I am still trying to understand the difference between feeling sweet
and feeling thankful.
if I were to ask your inquisitive mind, what would you tell me?
open your mouth, no words come out,
change your mind,
as your lips part,
the difference between the two is
I am incredibly thankful for your sweetness
because without your honey,
I wouldn't be the
bee's knees.

sunburn
Natalya Jean

this kind of wind is dangerous—
stealing the evening heat from your cheeks
before you even suspect a burn.

i however
know i'm feeling this summer sun
beating down on my swaying head
      unearthing motifs better left alone
      left buried
      (settled in the dirt long ago)
now cultivating these seasonal blooms.
i'm feeling something, for sure,
sweltering in this metaphorical greenhouse.

too blinded by the glare
of white teeth glinting in the sunlight
piercings flashing
tattoos tanning
to notice summer had arrived.
this weather flushes out everything, it seems—
limbs exposed
feelings exposed

i'm sweating, sitting here
across from you
slowly turning red
and waiting for autumn to begin.

Becoming

Lyndsay deManbey

Where are your lips
If I could find,
Taste the tickling whispers
And the soft wines?
A world of becoming
In your embrace,
Hug the blue shades
Of a pale moon sky;
Words between seats
Reveal our lives,
Laugh at the lights—
The hours have shifted.
Where have they gone,
Your eyes and mine?
Manta Rays with sunny veins
And golden cookie crumbs!

Processing Being
Chris Lindahl

or when your limbs are split
in two and your uphill battle becomes
your best-friends worst nightmare.
The thought of you
or the weight of your shoulders
buckling for full-blown catastrophe
is very hard to extract.

Realization given:
we must bury this deranged lovechild of ours.
Careless errors have brought
two and two together.
And based on quickly calculations,
this carousel is stopping.
But before you up and leave,
remember how arithmetic is not
what we thought it's meant to mean.

A Lesson in the Art of Love
Zoe Barnstone-Clark

I've been brought into the discovery of love
through summer orange trees,
and almond eyes colored sun-flecked gold
that leave the taste of wealth in my mouth.
I dwell in that fullness,
in the warm, buzzing home I constructed
For myself, within myself, with doors and windows left open for you.
I lose nothing of myself
in the gift (in the joy) of opening living space for you.
It is not empty space if its filled with all that is alive in you.

In our discovery of love
we uncover hidden cracks,
step upon untouched land,
unravel tangled knots
within ourselves, in all that surrounds us, in fullness, in togetherness.
In the power and possibility of love to at once
makes us one and remain strong as two.

Sweet Perennials
Ty Muto

Morning still dark blue
Sun breaks through flagging orange
Open to all things

Sweet perennials
Have historical wisdom
To begin again

Your blue-green glances
My heart skips double-dutch beats
Caught in your rhythm

What You Mean to Me
Melinda Cynthia Victoria Taylor

What you mean to me
Is hard to put into words
I fear but desire the potential to be
With you in every way possible
What you mean to me
Is what sunshine means to flowers
I just want to make you see
That I've spent countless hours
Thinking, hoping, imagining, fantasizing
What you mean to me
Has nothing to do with my imperfections
But more with who I am and want to be
And I need you to help me
And I need you to need me
What you mean to me
Is to have a dream come true
The opportunity
To really, truly, passionately love you
What you mean to me
Is so important and powerful
That to lose you would be
Such a tragedy
What you mean to me
Is friendship, truth, beauty, love
A future that I don't want to imagine
Unless you are an essential part of it.

Bring Me Home
for Malik
Smith E. Umland

Arabic like a silk road
touches my sun-scared skin
and I feel alight.
In honeycomb, toffee, and caramel
I find my refuge

My mouth waters easily
and you taste like gingerbread, oranges and
baklava every time I kiss you,
no matter how long it's been since you've brushed your teeth
or how many cigarettes you've smoked
You kiss me coffee
and teach me the value of late nights and early mornings

You are
every happiness I never thought I
would get to have
You are
a look of love
through whiskey-brown eyes
that fills my heart in such a way
I know I'll never be empty again,
no matter what the future becomes
You are
Arabic like a silk road
that brings me home.

mymoonmylover
Jake Tringali

the moon. she wore black. she made me nervous.

years ago, my travels and studies through astronomy introduced me to the moon proper. prior, the moon had been an acquaintance, someone i'd seen while walking through boston night after night. just another familiar face.

and so I was making new friends. jupiter and his massive fiery cousin sol, the way-out oort cloud, little venus cute-as-a-button. the gothic moon, pale and bright, was taking classes in human psychology. our first conversation was on a chilly january night. she kept her secrets but night after night, invited me back, as she slowly illuminated her private world.

i studied her shape, measured her librations. i ran my fingers along her provocative topography. she swung across the earth at her own pace, and i revolved around her, hungry for more.

dizzying, days were lost, and in a dark speck of time, i learned my orbit was false, and i was flung away a mere eight months later, another victim of celestial mechanics.

and then from time to time, without even looking, i would see her ghost. her phantom followed me from one city to another.

you can't capture the moon, not with gravity, not even with these words

she is the only one that could make me nervous, and i still measure my time in her terms.

Her Eyes Are Filled with Pain
Ellen Orell

Armor that enhances
The color of her eyes,
Cannot shield forever
What she feels inside.

Eyes that tell her secrets—
They're a passage to her heart.
It's clear she still loves him
But knows it's time to be apart.

Eyes that look so broken,
Like they're made of dusty glass—
Fragile in their rawness.
Her mind is on the past.

Memories that are happy.
She still laughs the same.
Her eyes betray her truth
Because they're glazed with pain.

Armor that has failed
No longer has a need,
So now she can be real.
Her pain is on her sleeve.

Here and Eternity
Ainsley Margaret Carman

Kiss me softly
And whisper into my bones
That love will know me
As I have known music is a fine wine
That ages with the soul

I pray to the tides and the falling sun
That you dance me through the chapters of our lives
That intertwine like spiral stair cases and the libraries of books
That seem eternal in their wisdom

The dust that settles on their spines

Look at me with eyes that reach for eternity
And arms that hold me
Here and now
A place I continue to struggle to be

And be with me
For just tonight
And convince me that eternity
Can become reality
With the softest stare
And the gentlest touch

Beauty

Because I am human and I am drawn to power,
Because I want to see Nature at her strongest,
Because I want to feel humbled, because I want to feel whole,
because I want to witness her.

- Callie Ann Marsalisi

Sagarmāthā / Chomolungma

Callie Ann Marsalisi

Everest is female,
And one day I want to see her up close,
Watch her rise into clouds and storms,
Her cold and her cols breaking waves in the blue-gray air,
Mother Nature showing off her daughter.

I want to stand by her side and live the feeling of
The pulse of the cold, ever-living rock.
Bare skin pressed,
For a brief, stupid second,
Against dirt and ice I hope will outlive me.

And I am not alone in my tenacity; somehow
The sight of a mountain ripping into our sky
Triggered an instinct in the collective mind
That brought all of us to say,
"I can be taller."

And we looked to a future on high
And with push and pull we learned
To work with a beast that gives and takes
In her own sure and secret way,
Passive and precise and beyond our understanding.

And I want to see her for all the same reasons
That hundreds want to stand brief and disoriented on her peak.
Because I am human and I am drawn to power,
Because I want to see Nature at her strongest,
Because I want to feel humbled, because I want to feel whole, because I want to
witness her.
Because she's there.

Starlight
Fitz Fitzgerald

The starlight had never looked so bright
Not in the sky, but in the reflection in your eyes
As you stared straight up, you'd never seen them before
The stars, not like this
You always were self-conscience about your eye color
But at this moment
On this big rock
Seemingly being swallowed by the trees
Except for the cliff dropping out on the westward end
As I sit here, looking at you
Brown is the perfect color for your eyes
It does the best job of reflecting that starlight
Straight from the heavens into your eyes.
Then bouncing off like a kaleidoscope of stars
Reflecting that starlight into mine.
I could get lost looking into your eyes

You look up into the night sky and say, "Doesn't it look so beautiful?"
And I just look straight at you and say
"Yes, she does."

You see, those things you thought about yourself
They don't matter here
The books, the papers, the tests
They're all the same
They just get more difficult as the years progress
But I swear as we snuck over that fence
Crawled through the bushes
And ran through the trees
As you lost your balance on that stray tree limb
And stumbled into me
In that moment of silence
When I caught you mid-fall
You dropped your theoretical text books and just held onto me
For once in your life you were set free

This silence isn't the silence you're used to
Instead of slight eraser noises and test scribbles in the background, if you listen
closely
You can hear birds chirping a beautiful sound
Mixed in with the crickets cricking away
And bushes blowing in the wind
Whistling through the leaves

And the only thing I think is that
I hope you never leave

We can just sit here on this big rock
Trees on all sides, with our feet hanging over the drop in front of us giving us a
view of the whole valley
The nighttime fog rolling in from the west
The symphony of nature, put perfectly on tempo
With your heart beating in your chest
I swear I could sit and watch the stars through your eyes all night

Raven or Crow
Jessica Imbro

Six months ago, she wilted into a pile of sheet music
and coffee beans and dew. I watched her hair float
out across the floor, reaching for the door but getting
caught in the cracks between the floor boards. She cries out but
it's too late, I cannot bring her back.
Her gelatin being burns a hole through to the gates
of Hades and she has left me, once a lover now
a melody floating between the hairs on my neck, running
its fingers over my chest,
telling me I was worth it, that I deserved it. My
body sublimed, I am a whisper between your fingertips,
I am a desperate wheeze in the ceiling of
the oldest house on the block with rust in the pipes and
dust coating the picture frames and
vines a sheath over the front door. You
are the urge to curl my fingers, you are the soreness and
the drop of warm sweat on my brow, dripping down my cheek.
It was a long journey.
You built a house around my sentience but halfway through you gave
up on following the blueprints and started
doodling on the walls, pasting colored paper onto my chest.
You made up symbols and carved them into my bones and here I
am, alive. They told you that you couldn't make up symbols and you said
that all symbols were made up, all of them.
You said everything was made up,
you said you and I were made up, us, and everyone.
A bird flew out of your mouth as you spoke. I caught it
in my hand and skinned it, fed it
to the fishes but kept the feathers, glued them to our insides.
You started whispering in blank verse. I draped your body in
black silk and left you to rot.

mirror meditation at some point past 2
Christina Smith

i feel most beautiful after the first failure of
the night when the journaling won't help and
the dinner has long since passed through i suddenly
become pleased by the half of my face illuminated by
my bedside lamp but why at this moment am i thrown
a cheekbone why is each hair on my brow suddenly
a cleansweep just why does my skin decide to paint itself for
me now? true it never asks me to stab a pencil into my flesh, it does
not need me to cavity another cream around and around
and leave behind a gnarled dimple but that still does not explain
why when i am so far removed from parading i
gaze and see someone who will one day run her fingers through another's
hair as an afterthought. i know there's no gaze but
my own here and i at least know the reasons for
that, my stubby fingernails remind me of that my
baggy bedshirt reminds me of that but i can't let this clarity
descend not when i can still work for myself even
the logo on my front that i am so fond of smothers the
growling. and eventually i try the night on again and it feels
nice on my thighs even though the promise of the
next glance on the way to the cereal bowl keeps
me awake for longer than it should.

Giacomina
Michael Christopher DiClemente

The square

    was beautifully lit

She descended

    the awkward stairway

In a way

    that was marvelously unique

As I looked up to catch a glimpse

    in such a way that would not disturb her elegance

That was the angel

    with whom I will spend the rest of my days

Shh
Mia Mazzaferro

I can't hear anything.
My ears are full of flower petals.
Of your rose-turned voice,
tilting the balance
I've so carefully calibrated.

The sound of you
muffles sweet all other sharpness.
Velvet flush—
Do you know what warm knives sound like?

The swollen bloom of you in my ears
—I blush full-body.
I am knocked down
and shadow-wrapped
Tripping over your voice's vines.

The world is a hum
of deafening softness.

You are loudest when you whisper.

Nature, Wildlife, and the Outdoors

"Never has the air so quickly immersed itself in psalm.
Never so blue those nights of red leaves,
so hollowed of their pigment, half-decayed and thin"

- *Alessandra Miranda*

The Pine
Eleonora Mortillaro

he sits under a pine tree—the one with the
rope swing—on the bank of the river behind our house.
just being a man with nothing else to do except
look at a sky that has no images in the clouds.

he wonders how wonder can die without
mourning—forgotten—in changes and growing pains. until,
too late. it turns bitter, the sweet red blood
of the mammal that can kill its own instincts.

he is under a pine tree, and in the earth,
words are made with a broken bottle he found in the ferns:
twenty years ago, the rope wasn't frayed. there wasn't glass in the dirt.

at least not as much.

The Sailor's Mistress

Timothy Chambers

He is young, naïve, and bold
She is strong, wild, and free
Her powers are ancient and cold
He should learn to let her be

He is a fool, nothing but a dreamer
She will buck him like a wild mare
He knows he could never tame her
Yet it's her he could never forswear

He can never underestimate her
Her mood is forever changing
She is the strongest force of mother nature
But she's his whole being

Nothing can separate the sailor from his mistress: the sea
That is how it has always been and will always be.

Stitches

Julia DesCamp-Renner

There's this jagged scar above my knee in the shape of the tree limbs
that ripped across the sky on the night last December
when my best friend told me I needed to learn to let go. There's a story behind it
that I'd tell if I could remember; it's from a fall down a slope in an Arkansas cave,
or a canoe that flipped in the foggy aftermath of a hurricane,
or a poorly judged jump into a river on the west coast of Ireland
during the summer when coasts started to blur together and everything I'd learned
about Pangea
started to make sense. There's a story behind it,
but the only part I can remember is that even now
I look at beautiful things and think,
this is going to cut deep enough to leave a scar.

Everyone Was Elephants
-After Matthea Harvey
Marina Starkey

All around us were the anachronisms
of the animal kingdom. Beluga whales
burped like a bundle of bees. Baby ears
broke like baboons. Carl confessed
he was just a cicada. He couldn't figure out
why most of his cousins were crushed.
Danger continued to study us, but he never
understood why we were so deeply
damaged. Eons ago, I explained,
everyone was elephants. Early mornings
were the easiest: feeding was at four,
we floated as freely as the fire,
and we couldn't fathom how anyone needed
two hands, two feet. But as it goes, the germs
got us. Geologists didn't get it—
How much hair? How many fingers?
We didn't know what to say. It all happened
in an instant. Jokes were told to justify
the jaundice. Journalists jotted down
the journey. Kites were given to the koalas
as a consolation prize. Listening was the hardest.
Long hours were spent locating our earlobes,
but the lovers had it the worst. Many attempts
were made to ameliorate the maze,
but nobody knew how to navigate—we never
thought we needed to.
One of us tried answering for our outrage,
but all she said was *open*.

Purposefully, the new people
began to purge their pessimism. Life became quaint.
The unanswerable question was quantified.
Religion was re-appropriated. Right and wrong
were established. Shortly, the Sahara was missed,
so the specialists prescribed us aspirin. We talked
about returning to the trees, but talk was talk was talk.
Our memory was useless. Misunderstanding
the unexpressed became the usual. Violets were planted
for our valentines, and we've been living within these weeks
for weeks. We don't know why we X out
all the days. Xenophobia remains,
but Zelda believes the zebras have it all figured out.

White Caps
Henry P. Gray

Standing on the shore, staring off under your cap, you think to yourself
What do those white sprouting sea flowers mean?
Like white sprinkles of salt blown across the ocean's surface
Jumping over the horizon on a calm day, making a seaman nervous
No two alike, no two similar, but all intimately connected
With spines stretched throughout the ocean, but without an end
Scaring off those who know better, and welcoming a man of a humorous blend

Cold Water
Samuel Henry Penney

I stand at a window overlooking the garden
The Maine breeze lapping at me
Like the waves of the Atlantic
In my mind I slowly step onto the windy shore
My ankles go numb.

I turn my gaze low to the pinks and yellows
The marvelous whites and greens
I whisper to myself in my head
The haughty words I'll write about this moment
Hoping I'll remember them another time.

The rustle of leaves
The crash of water on sand
What difference is there?
I am up to my chest in both
My trunk goes numb.

Hills here roll as gently as eggs in a nest
A curve molded by a mother's hand
Their grassy hides shiver in the ocean
Reminding us of something long forgotten
It almost becomes too much.

The leaves break on the sand
The sea spills over the garden
Mother's symphony cries out
My head goes numb.

Gratitude Jar
Lindsey Bressler

There is a place I know
that smells like mouse droppings and challah bread rising in the
oven and cilantro and sage,
a place that is as close to the heartland as it is far
from the skyline,
where if you squint just before 7 o'clock on a Saturday
evening, you'll find not three nor one but two clouds up above
and where chickens pose regally for their portraits upon
thrones of eggshells.

In Hebrew, the name of God
is too sacred for a human mouth
so we draw it with our hands instead,
tucking dirt into the cracks beneath our fingernails while
holding each other up atop ladders
worried that if we speak too quickly,
we'll miss the subtlety.

The Arabic words for *bullshit* and
for *freedom* are separated by a difference the size of a blade of grass.
A difference the same distance apart as the Hebrew
word for *soul*, and the Arabic word for *breath*.

Proving that on the days when we choose to listen more, we
hear less.

Aware that warriors must train for peace with the
same intensity as they do for combat.
Aware that when we pull purple carrots then plant orange
ones that we all come from the same dirt.

In this place
without names for each other but the melodies
in our heads, I met two wise women.

The first collected all of my guilt in a heavy bucket
of leaves and gravel and handed it back to me,
breathy with effort, saying,
"Do you see these plants? How they no longer
have their roots in the earth? Dump it in the back of the truck. Do not
wonder after them. They're just weeds."

The first day I harvested beets I was

afraid to see how my hands shone like the
color of a deer's blood.

The second opened the gate to her garden and told
me the secret, the line resting parallel to
that single blade of grass.

You must find the balance between tender and tough.

Lighthouse
Madeleine Olson

i'm going to buy a lighthouse
so I can be the light to any boat
coming for the night

it'll be the kind with a candy cane
                    red spiral
                            ascending to
                                    the top
with a wide clear window
around the entire circumference
with me
as the tiny green cricket
inching close to the light like
i'm in some giant candle
aglow in this glassy watch room
up in its tippity
                    top
                        untroubled
                                tower

i'll sit there
criss-cross apple sauced
one hand resting on my eyebrows
peering into the night
into the black waves
            into the stolen sky

"click-click!"
See my flashlight light as lightning
capturing giant photos
with the bright beam blinking

"Ahoy!"
incoming they surge
            sailors resting on the voyage
                    sailors washed ashore
                            sailors coming home

i let the light remain
a steady warm glow
yellow spotlight on
the dancing waves
            the slapping waves

like claps in the dark

and i'll control the light night light
alone in the tower

solitude among the simple people / company among the alive waters

Necropolis
April Wildes

When I'm lonely
I take the trains
to places I don't know.

Jump off at random stops
on random lines
on the twisted map of the city.

I walk with eyes down
side-stepping cracked asphalt
and dog shit.

I see ants carrying dead ants
back to their nest,
I suppose.

One struggling with a crumb on its back,
its leg stuck
in melted tar.

A whole city under this city
full of ants,
the dead ones, too.

January
-After "10" by Inger Christensen
Alessandra Miranda

Through rubble a new year emerges
but is hardly heard, snow circling itself confused,
as gingerly as when ice is returned to water, a shift
as if asleep or by hands unknown. Jaundice

of the mind, grown sick of its remembering,
stuffed full of yellow leaves, remembering too soon
that fall exists, windbreakers, wind-burned lips,
those evolving skins that won't be shed for months

exist, in the burning hills
when purple exhausts itself.
Never has the air so quickly immersed itself in psalm.
Never so blue those nights of red leaves,

so hollowed of their pigment, half-decayed and thin;
never have I been so sure that what didn't happen
still wouldn't. January, you are not autumn, January,
your unfolding chill and bareness exist,

half a year's rest and ruin before
change so changing and steps so instep
with the expectant weather, expecting rain, and sun
sinking, sinking like a glowing blossom

into earth. Earth in its speechless resolve
amid slow time exists, Earth on liminal
between dark and stars, Earth in its house
with its cold dust and cracking oak, oak trees, palm trees,

palms held tight pressed, prayer, something angry, something desperate
to sing to god. And to wait for an answer
in the streets, a moonless tide, with summer
a heavy memory and the shadow
of blue-burned snow on the roadside.

121

Crepuscular
Claire Benson

The edges of the grass turn both
transparent and opaque as the day-star
imbibes in its slow descent
slowly slipping
beneath the foothills.

The grass sucks up the remaining light,
burning orange and a radical red.

Some nights the Sun resists subordination
and subjugates the darkening sky
with reds and pinks and oranges
as the Moon rises, heaving
a cratered body nearer
to its nighttime perch.

The moment
the Sun and Moon are equal

in the sky, one's face illuminating
the other's illuminated,
twilight is actuated and the
air is crepuscular and tense
and the grass is enflamed.
Now, the Moon accepts

inevitable blindness
begotten by perceived equality.

Red
Kayleigh Turgeon

I remembered the squirrel that I'd seen,
the red one, but not her gritty haste.
Like a fish, anxious, darting at serpentine
speed, not with the grays' loping peaceful pace.

Crouching, tail flat to back, unyielding, still,
then pouncing unafraid into the air,
her feathery tail frenzies overhill
To her burrow beneath the trees somewhere

In the leafy shadows. Clenched in vice-like teeth,
the prized butternut glows green, jealously
guarded. Emerging again from beneath,
she flies to defend her territory.

But blind to her fierceness, I saw softness,
in such strength seen only precious smallness.

The Day the Rain Blew Sideways
Brittany Frederick

Mama always said that the thunder and lightning
scared her, not because of the rain, not the lightning
but because that first clap of thunder came up out of nowhere.

The day the rain blew sideways
was just another day, I had lunch,
combed out my kinky hair, and set to work on my primer
but by three o' clock in the afternoon

the rain was angrily slappin' our windows,
it sounded like someone knockin' on the door asking for
forgiveness, it sounded like when you drop a couple of pots
and they clang several times before coming to a dented stop.

I sat in the basement because it felt like the very air was angry,
the sky was grey and heaving itself onto us all.
That was the day when the maple tree in our front yard

launched itself from the soil as if to fly
before crashing sideways over the picket fence that divided
our house from the one several yards away.

Mama always said the Lord could make equals of us all
and he would when the time had come.

Inspiration

"On the other side of the glass, I stand alone.
I howl—it just echoes back: *Break out, fly!* Repeat."

- Natalia Perkins

Rise with the Sun
Natalia Perkins

Gray pajamas, staring at a screen. Sigh, repeat.
Miles until you touch those dimpled hands. Say bye, repeat.

He loves you in the wrong ways. Your mother doesn't know.
Look at her like an ancient jade mirror, lie, repeat.

On the other side of the glass, I stand alone.
I howl—it just echoes back: *Break out, fly!* Repeat.

I count your scars and turn away, a horse with blinders.
I try to keep on living. Slip on shoe, tie, repeat.

They say you can't solve the labyrinth, only give up.
That's not why we rise with the sun: to die, repeat.

There are roads that keep going, stars we cannot see.
Even your mind's folds span forever. Why repeat?

Natalia is a foreign name to you, I know.
But we're both made of stardust. Let's defy repeat.

Ascension
Keelan Murphy

Flowing through these veins is capacity
But my hands tremble far too much to progress
In this mind is the profound will
But my head is too considerably clouded by the discharge of unsolicited thoughts
In this chest is the raw intensity of passion
But my heart hysterically thrashes far too dauntingly to draw breath
"Step forward," they say. "Just do it." As if it's just as elementary as that swoosh on our sneakers
But what is "it?" The call to action requires a response, but the first step is always the most ambitious
And I'm often caught between questioning which direction is best to go
and where I even presently reside
Too late I grasp that stillness is an undesirable though recognized answer
In these veins, I had the capacity
But I kept my hands idle
In this mind, I had the will
But I locked it away in my head, attempting to keep the monsters within at bay
In this chest, I had the passion
But I suppressed my heart into submission
And yet just as we must, time continues to trek on
what could have been is ashes
but I choose to grant myself the serenity to ask, what is yet to be?
And realize it's born from those very same remains.
When the sun rises, so will I, and rather than lifting all the mountains,
Perhaps I'll simply climb them
one step at a time.

How to Play Piano
Samantha Parker

Inhale.
Find the music that makes your heart sing.
The music that tickles your heart strings,
that resonates with you.
Challenge yourself.
Find a piece that stretches your mind as well as your fingers.
Sit down.
Breathe:
Inhale, exhale.
Inhale, exhale.
Roll back your shoulders, slowly, deliberately.
Sit up nice and tall, as if tied to a pole.
Balance a crown on your head.
Lift up your arms; they are lead branches extending from your body,
your fingers quick moving feathers on the keys,
flying as if still attached to birds.
Rest your fingertips, gently, on the keys, brushing them softly,
like touching a pond without making a ripple.
Exhale again, and on the inhale, begin.
Emotion flows through your fingertips,
raw and powerful. Vibrations of sound reverberate,
tangible in your chest.
Close your eyes, let muscle memory take over and whisk you away.
Your hands know what to do.
Slowly rock back and forth to the rhythm of your heart and the melody.
Float down the river of song.
Feel chills of sorrow or joys warmth in every key your fingertips kiss.
Wake up; you have gotten too lost, your fingers started to float down the river with you,
but they cannot, for they have a job to do.
You cannot swim across an ocean and stop halfway.
Music is a piece of soul, fragile and so easily destroyed by the untrained hand.
Butterflies, the notes flit from measure to measure,
Twist around themselves,
Spiral through restraining bars.
Beethoven, Marianelli, Debussy, Rachmaninoff.
Masterminds who carved out a piece of their heart and put it on a page, just for you.
Pound in anger, flow in sorrow, tickle in joy, kiss in love,
your fingers on the ivory tell their story out loud, for the world to hear.
Treasure your ability to translate for them.
Exhale.

Architect
Cody Marx

Here is darkness, Here is sadness.
It is four thick walls, steel bars
That close around me, cage me in.
It has no comfort, no sleep,
No escape. Here has only him.

He is anger, torture.
He is cunning, convincing,
Shielding me from the hell
I would surely meet outside,
He says. Sometimes I believe him.

He is my mirror image,
He who built this jail for me.
I am his secret to keep,
The shadow he can't shake.
I am his cross to bear.

He keeps me Here, alone,
In his house of lies, of shame.
He locks me up in this prison
Away from truth, from freedom,
From a life worth living.

His thoughts are mine and I hear him.
I feel his weakness, his anger,
His fear that I will ruin him,
Ruin the life he has planned.
But through him I see There.

There is open, There is warm.
It is a bright, boundless world
That wants me to live, to thrive.
It has happiness, love, hope,
And There is worth fighting for.

Stickers Don't Smudge
Liza Brackbill

I remember when I wrote on my laptop—
and I remember what I wrote
and I remember everyone being kind of outraged
not because of what I wrote
but because I wrote anything at all
on my laptop
and I thought this was pretty funny
because everyone puts stickers on their laptops,
and writing on one did not seem more destructive
to me

I want to go my own way without causing a scene
I don't want to follow the crowd
but I don't want to be destructive, either
I want to help, but I can't

Last Thursday,
my boyfriend told me
that I shouldn't wear my favorite jean jacket
when we're together anymore
so that night, I instead wore my favorite jean vest,
and he broke up with me
and I cried,
but I only cried for a short time
and on Saturday, when my tears dried,
I went out wearing my favorite jean jacket
and no one was there to tell me anything about it that I didn't want to know

and I was sitting at the bar
among strangers, lots of them,
by myself, and for some reason I thought of my laptop
and I started thinking,

it's pretty funny
that the writing I did
eventually smudged right off

I Don't Pray
Caleigh Grogan

Follow along the thicket of brambles,
move up and over the hills, slide
tirelessly down the valleys, through water
or dark red mud; move,
however you must, to follow the star.

Wiser men than you have lost
their way across the plains, or
they've died of thirst beneath the moon.
An angel will not guide you
to a virgin's holy womb, nor will praying
promise safe passage. You are as alone

as any voyager who's ever sought
to learn something. Leave your pleading
and your desperation far behind.
Once you've crested the mountain, once
you've touched the star
with your hands or your lips or your tongue,
you need only look below
and speak words of praise for the place
where we all began.

Miscellaneous

Do not guard your faint heart,
Without the help of my sword.
For I'd lend it a hundred times over
To ensure your safe recovery.

- Paul Horte

Indehiscent//Drupe
Divya Kirti

I don't get to be weak. There are
no fault lines in my body.
I don't get the option to
break open as I grow;
I split from seam to seam when I
ripen. There is nothing inside me
that I am willing to release.

All I have is whatever is left
of me after they ravage
my flesh and plant my pit
in the loose soil
in the groves

where the others before me
were forced to grow too.

Skin
Shem Elias Tane

I am a collection of bruised elbows
and stubbed toes.
Skin scabbed and
two rows
of buck teeth.

Mumbled over apostrophes
and hyperboles.
Too timid to burp
yet speak.

I will never be one of you
sitting here looking at pretty colors,
wishing you didn't have so much attitude.

Cupped lips
holding back adolescent lies.
Foolish hands on a December night,
while your sister's cough tightens.
Swearing that you would be home before midnight,
maybe not.

I know the twisted irony found
with the mark of ink on my skin
that some would claim no shame.
Do you not remember ashes and mass graves?

The memories will be all that's left.
The stories we have to tell,
the good along with the bad.

Winter Streets from Here
James Holbert

then for all the world
seasons tinkled high as stars
sometimes do singing

fortified fences
fall forever not ever
in madam's spring

it brings little weeks
where good boys learn the ganges
dipping their toes in

Wind
Cole David Vick

Turning tumbling biting the skin from my teeth
Ripping through sonic landscapes
Sunken in police sirens and citizens' yells
Too cold out for the likes of me
I can't be expected to brave the world
For you or anyone else
I can only be expected to brave it for myself
But the hinges on my door are broken
And my boots are getting old
And my coat's in the car
And I need some more coffee grounds
Maybe I'll stitch myself up
And try next week
Patchwork man walking down the street
Braving the world for no one but
Himself

Our Shy Sun
Donari Yahzid

We reign under a shy sun. When it doesn't burn too fierce, we remove more clothes. We touch up
on each other, welcoming some warmth. Our shy sun peers over the water to watch us play. Our
shy sun makes others retreat. We let it peek at us for entertainment. We are not ones who take in
its rays; we are full. When we tire, we watch it blush hues of mango peals. It crouches deep into
the sea, blending its light with blue. Cool winds tickle the trees into applause for the evening
show.

You See Venus in a Fur Coat
Allister Quilon

i see the glamorization
of beauty using
the skinning of beings
(robbed of "sentience")
for sport; ["sentience"="domestication"]
their ancestors
figured that's what
it takes to
make it

through the ice
cold win ter la la land so
ba black sheep, been
beaten down for this;
never had a chance, melt
clean into snow, entrenched in dirt;
where the river been
dammed, got your fingers
in the ground, got your
sand in the toes,
took your heartbreak hotel
cigarette blues, made a
pretty little portrait,
wear you like a tattoo
i'm sayin', i'm sayin'

where they put the good news?
do they hide it in the cellar?
do they hide in the brews?
we're the cool kids, cool
kiss death in twos, we've
been running out of love,
we've been running on the fumes
i'm sayin', i'm sayin'

all i see is bad shit, all
i see is lip service paid,
the calming of the masses,
i see the ashes,
bottom of the star bucks
bottle all the kids on the street
been catching all the ashes,
chain smoking like freedom's nothing
more than the minimum we cash in

Hell

Sierra Diaz

They'll say "love"
I'll spit on the ground where they walk
That word
Covering up my wounds
"Who cut you?"
His eyes, concerned
Lighting up
The stupid little lanterns
Hah! I'll laugh
"You"

The Cure
Narsimha Chintaluri

My mind may mend when I repent
Dark thoughts lost in the midst of salvation
Bright lights fight as I make the ascent
Into the heavens, lost in translation

Inspiration must first be found
Before one can claim that it was lost
Not every talent is renowned
Not every challenge is worth the cost

I pressed my pen pensively against paper
Trying to cope without my crutch
Ever since my habits have been tapered
I feel as if I've lost my touch

But old habits are hard to break I hear
And I fear near here they will reappear

The Green-Eyed Monster
Deanna Haas

one morning I wake up and notice tangles in my hair,
and I find my tiny bluebird stuck in one of the snares
I don't know what to do so I jump out of bed
to examine the little creature stuck on my head
I am brushing my teeth with some Colgate blue
when I notice something funny about my eyes
once-hazel irises have turned a bright emerald shade
and beneath my right arm, I find my crimson heart
then I remember that my poor little bird is stuck
and the fight we got into the previous night
it was really a silly argument, you might say, but
I had to know who it was he was texting that day
and all ended well once we fell asleep
I reach with a gentle hand and let him down
and he chirps and hops right by my feet
when I see that some little robin has favorited his tweet
all of a sudden I feel a rumble somewhere
and licking my lips, I turn to the little bird
and snatch him up before he can say a word

Then I swallow him whole, I regret to say.
He can't—he won't be the one to get away.

walking poem
Anisha Pai

a leaf falls on my head
& I fall into the pockets of my skirt
tugging at the bottom of my belly
pulling the yolk of my head
tugging at the bottom of my
crop top. nevermind.
back in the sun, a shoe slips off
a piece of a shoe slips off into the soil & I wonder
how sharp the ridges of my toe must be to
cut at my grandmother's own sandals
she cuts at her own sandals
[the sound your tongue makes when you pull it from the roof of your mouth]
melarie she owns sandals, melarie
she says she doesn't do it for the spiritual shit

she says she's spiritual, shit,
the leaves are already brown between my toes
& I want to stop looking at my feet but
now there are tree roots between them & now
I am in shade: calm / calmly tugging at
the bottom of a tree. The space inside my
head is more pumpkin than persona &
the trees are running conspiracies down my spine;
the wind is warning my belly
about how small clovers can become- they can hide
the 4th leaf in my own mouth, a mouse, a vole,
a rat keeps running into crowded parks away
from the home it made in the ground & a ridge
in my toe keeps wearing holes into the pockets of my skirt.

Echo of Small Things
Randy Rowe

Your music is the universe,
floating dust sifting time.

Melancholy but pleasurable,
opaque yet luminous.

I stoop in confinement,
but listen to the vastness of space.

It soars heavenly downward,
droning upward from the void.

Bell stars faintly touch perception,
glowing root tones hold sway.

In your power, I soothe.
In your absence, I awake.

Falling
Paul Horte

To push and to pull.
To climb and to succeed.
Falling and failing; those were always options.

Dare I breathe everlasting words,
Forgetting to remind myself of self-worth.
Don't remind me of my failures.
They don't fail to remind me.

Each Autumn I'm reminded
Of the horrible memories I made.
Each year that passes,
Digs myself a deeper grave.

Words so blatant, I might spell it out for you,
Though I fear it might fall on flat ears.
You've already discovered l'exquisite douleur.
Perhaps if I would sing it rather than spell it,
You might hear sounds you'd never heard,
Or contemplate life in new shades you'd never seen.

But for the rest of them,
They know we crave serenity in forms we can't understand.
Safely biding time to lure us from that which we are learning to fathom.
It feels sickly, and like you've arrived home after a long vacation.
It feels like you're a pile of dirt waiting to be dug.

Speaking everlasting words,
Finding control on hopeless wanderer,
Singing everlasting tones.
Binding a heart of hopeless romantic.
Dream of worlds that do not exist on this plane.

Do not guard your faint heart,
Without the help of my sword.
For I'd lend it a hundred times over
To ensure your safe recovery.
Though I'd lent it far too many times
To guard what I thought was divinity,
I'd gladly protect your uncertain light.

She was suicide,
And you were dying.

They counted my failures,
We counted our victories.
Falling and failing,
Those were never options.

Shadows
Rick Faletto

I'm drawn by the mystery in shadows.
Forest paths dappled with shimmering, warm light
but with the coolness of the wet leaves—
The coursing energy that emanates from the living soil
into the soles of my feet
and then courses in me.
emanates
from me.

And when the earth is all shadow,
its easy, unrushed breath
draws chilly through my skin
as ever it permeates all,
breathing like the forest,

delicate and enchanting, like
a million morning snowflakes
drifting without direction.
Invigorating,
a gentle shiver
like those delivered
by moments that transcend our biology.

The cool embrace of starlight
Crystallized in the midnight dew.

The soft embrace present when
      uncertain and wild
      like a crystal-eyed child
      we dance to the rhythm of eternity,
living echoes tumbling in the chaos

spinning under stars of primordial skies—
the breeze in communion
with our rapturous sighs.

Exhaust
Jennifer Morgan

Waking up
exhausts me. I breathe the carbon monoxide
and ignore the alarm and the neighbors'
screams. Smoke
pours in like sunlight through the wonky shades
but I don't want to see it. I just want
to be a vegetable. I never want
to stand again, rot from green.
Mostly I'm green
like a soldier with a red
badge of courage on his back.
I read a Tumblr post where a girl said
she regretted coming in to herself every morning.
I sleep past noon and it isn't enough.
T-swift doesn't have enough advice
for girls like me who sometimes like girls
and sometimes get heartbroken for no reason at all.
Eventually I'll get tired of being
tired and go outside,
not squinting this time. Open
the wonky shades and let them clatter to the floor.

Mourning
Simi Esan

In the velvet before morning
you will learn—
all synastry is potential.
What could be will not.
You cannot give what you do not have,
and it was not your abundance but his lack.

Prometheus in Baltimore
Montgomery Alcott

The upper thigh was open, pink and yellow,
Its emanations foul and intimate.
Thrushes, finches, mockingbirds and tits
Undid the knots.

It looks in lamplight like some smith or fire
Burned a design on the naked dirt.
The man on the rock keeps secret
Before he goes to cash the unnamed check.

The Chicken Life

James Robotham

A hundred shining eyes;
black pebbles on the ocean floor,
dissolved into darkness.
Bodies jostle like padded linebackers
swollen, greasy, moshing to distorted shrieks.
caws elicited from beak stabbings.
Stampeding feet slap like smacking lips
on fresh, warm shit—icing on the
devil's food, hardened and stale
in ancestral layers, lakes
of steaming piss engulf the bathers,
legs snapping under the crushing weight
of bodies growing larger, feet dangling,
wriggling in a desperate backstroke, longing
for escape, a matter of light and death.

Husk
Emily Rosello Mercurio

A night rain beats the windows,
pushes a tree to the ground.
I am writing you a poem
on curls of garlic paper.

The poem rasps, odorous,
a minced head pressed
by the side of a knife.
It rains and rains in my kitchen.

Heavy drops collect on the ceiling,
skitter down the walls, splash the stove.
The hot oil cracks, splashes back.
The burner flashes blue in the breeze.

The oven's black chamber
fills with rain. The door leaks.
An acid water, it could dissolve knives,
given enough time.

The garlic husks float on the flood,
white sails with narrow veins.
The smell never fades. Underwater
the ink melts, clouds itself away.

Furnace
Domenic J. Scopa

Like depression,
there seems to be no origin,

and that's what draws attention to the sound,
a low grumble, subtle as a former lover
captive so securely in your memory
she might as well be in another country,
where the native language is as foreign
as the dialects of raindrops.
Is this what it's like to listen so attentively to a heartbeat,
its persistence like a bass drum doomed to repetition,
musical notations playing out your death,
and though you don't know where,
tonight someone will groan
while staring at the shoreline of a razor's edge,
wishing for a slice to end it all,
and a married man will mumble reconciliation
to an old flame on the phone,
and perhaps something as simple as thunder, too?
But you don't recognize that grumble,
so stop acknowledging it;
it's midnight, just a diesel engine idling,
just a pit bull growling in a backyard,
just the throaty breathing of the furnace
you thought you had repaired.

Note to the Reader

We hope you enjoyed our publication! If you have, we ask that you please consider writing a brief review for the book on Amazon.com. In your review, be sure to mention the title of the poem (or the name of the poet) that you enjoyed the most—we will take reader reviews heavily into account when it comes time to decide who will be invited to the nationwide edition of this series in 2018!

About Z Publishing House

Begun as a blog in the fall of 2015, Z Publishing, LLC, has since transitioned into book publishing. This transition is in response to the problem plaguing the publishing world: For writers, finding new readers can be tremendously difficult, and for readers, finding new, talented authors with whom they identify is like finding a needle in a haystack. With Z Publishing, no longer will anyone will anyone have to go about this process alone. By producing anthologies of multiple authors rather than single-author volumes, Z Publishing hopes to harbor a community of readers and writers, bringing all sides of the industry closer together.

To sign up for the Z Publishing newsletter or to submit your own writing to a future anthology, visit www.zpublishinghouse.com. You can also follow the evolution of Z Publishing on the following platforms:

Facebook: www.facebook.com/zpublishing
Twitter: www.twitter.com/z_publishing

Author Biographies

Montgomery Alcott
Montgomery is an alumnus of St. John's College.

MaKayla M Allen
MaKayla moved from upstate New York at 13 to grow up as a Cape Cod wash-a-shore. Now living in Boston, her writing parallels environment and identity to examine how both can change so often, and so easily.

Sharon Amuguni
Sharon is a poet residing in Somerville. As an immigrant and woman of color, much of her writing focuses on emotional and mental well-being, feelings of otherness, and the search for radical self-love. Sharon utilizes poetry as a cathartic tool for healing and reflection. She hopes to provide some sense of solace for other young women of color through her poetry.

Michael Anthony
A University of Massachusetts alumnus, Michael is influenced by imagism and sociology.

Erynne Arvisais
Erynne is a senior at Assumption College, majoring in psychology with a minor in human services. She was raised in Attleboro, Massachusetts. She enjoys horseback riding, reading, and spending time with friends and family. She hopes to start her career in human services and eventually attain an MSW.

Michael Baker
Michael is currently a student at the University of Massachusetts, Amherst and is just beginning to write poetry regularly. Follow his new poetry page Tempest in a Teacup on Twitter (TempestPoetry) and Instagram (tempestpoetry) for more content!

Megan Alyson Barnes
Megan analyzes gender norms and builds eccentric communities of friends at Wheaton College under the guise of studying sociology and women's and gender studies. She urges you to contact her at barnes_megan@wheatoncollege.edu if interested in reading more of her written run-ins with life in all of its strange glory.

Zoe Barnstone-Clark
Zoe is a junior at Mount Holyoke College in South Hadley, Massachusetts. The inspiration for her poetry is typically reading better writers than herself and/or any amount of emotional surplus in need of release.

Claire Benson
Claire is a poet who writes about the abstract, relationships, and time. Her favorite writings include John Keats's letters and John Irving's novels. She can be contacted at benson.claire.a@gmail.com.

Sarah Better
Sarah is a 19-year-old emerging poet born and raised in Quito, Ecuador. She currently studies psychology, writing, and music at Northeastern University in Boston.

Nicole Boliver
Nicole is a recent graduate of Franklin Pierce University with a major in English with a track in creative writing. She enjoys writing poems and stories in her free time. She loves to use her imagination in everything she does and hopes to share it with the world.

Liza Brackbill
Liza attends the University of Massachusetts, Amherst where she studies creative writing. She also enjoys hiking, biking, and playing the ukulele.

Lindsey Bressler
Lindsey is a senior at Northeastern University where she studies international affairs and economics. Her blog is lindseygoesto.wordpress.com. She is originally from Tucson, Arizona.

Eddie Brophy
Eddie is both a published poet and accomplished musician who resides in a suburb of Massachusetts with his wife and seven-month-old son, Dylan Thomas. Eddie's writing caters to a dark curiosity about the existential meaning of life, while coming to terms with all the detriments of that introspective thought process. Why are we so eager to die more than we are to live uninhibited and poisoned by fear?

Laura Cafasso

Laura is a soon-to-be graduate of Emerson College. She studied the ultimate trifecta: writing, literature, and publishing. Poetry is her passion, but she also enjoys writing movie reviews. Laura is originally from Franklin, Massachusetts.

Kyle Calise

Kyle is a poet, photographer, animator, and aspiring human being living in Boston.

Ainsley Margaret Carman

Like one of her professors, Ainsley believes we are wordsmiths and lovers of language. Writing has the capability to set minds on fire or to put them to rest. Ainsley turns to writing for both. Her works reflect her thoughts on nature, love, God, time, and writing.

Nicole Cerundolo

Nicole is an undergraduate psychology major at Northeastern University. Her love of writing has been an especially important part of her life ever since she was little, and she plans to continue pursuing her passion in her spare time.

Timothy Chambers

Timothy is a cadet at Massachusetts Maritime Academy. He grew up on the North Shore of Massachusetts, where he has been working for a deep-sea fishing company since 2012. He hopes that one day he can write while still pursuing a career at sea. He can best be contacted by email at timothy.chambers@maritime.edu.

Natasha Charest-Ciampa

Natasha is a student graduating from the University of Massachusetts in 2018. She can be reached by email at ncharestciam@umass.edu or through Facebook under the name Natasha Ciampa.

Narsimha Chintaluri

Narsimha wants to publish a book of poetry someday. And a novel. And create/write/direct a TV show. And a movie. Someday.

Lev Craig

Lev is a New York—based writer and theatre artist. They graduated from Harvard University in 2016 with an A.B. in English. Selected publications: *The Adroit Journal* (Editors' List, 2015 Prize for Poetry); *Architrave*. Recent theatre credits: *Pin* and the Blue Fairy* (The Brick: co-playwright/producer; Drama League: co-playwright). Lev can be reached via email at levpcraig@gmail.com.

Kimberly Dacorogna

Kimberly is a senior at Northeastern University where she studies English and theatre.

Davina Daines

Davina lives in Brooklyn with her wife and dog, Scout.

Maureen DeLeo

A native of Boston, Maureen has studied English at Stonehill College as well as Irish studies at NUI Galway. She is especially fond of the works of Dylan Thomas, Seán Ó Ríordáin, and WB Yeats. Travel, tea, and The Smiths are among her passions.

Lyndsay deManbey

Lyndsay is a second-year college student at BCC, where his poetry has been published in the campus literary magazine. He also performs theatre there as well as in and around the Berkshires. Generally, he tries to keep it chill, and poetry is what serves as a relaxing meditation for him.

Will deManbey

Will is your run-of-the-mill daydreamer, who enjoys poking and prodding the universe for its many secrets. He is not by any means a poet but combines words in such a way that occasionally resembles poetry. So, anything included here is nothing more than a happy accident.

Gaia DeNisi

Gaia is a sophomore at Williams College and is pursuing an undergraduate degree in English. Her poetry has been published in the Celebration of Poets anthologies and in the *Williams Literary Review*. Past issues of the *Williams Literary Review* can be accessed at williamslitreview.wordpress.com.

Julia DesCamp-Renner

Julia studies environmental science at Northeastern University in Boston. She has conducted ecological research in the San Juan Islands, New England, and Galway, Ireland, and draws inspiration for her poetry from her lifelong fascination with the natural world. She can be reached at www.juliarenner.net and julesmrenner@gmail.com.

Sierra Diaz

Sierra, an aspiring author of poetry and short stories, has a fondness for free verse poetry, Halloween, and green tea. She explores internal struggle through a unique voice, dark humor, and most certainly a bit of sarcasm. She can be contacted via email at sierradiazmarie@gmail.com.

Michael Christopher DiClemente

Michael is the loving father of two beautiful girls that provide him with inspiration every day. Michael's wife gives him support and an always keen eye to look over his work. Michael is a middle school history teacher. Michael has dabbled in poetry since high school.

Tim DiFazio

Tim is a fifth-year English/linguistics student at Northeastern University. He is an editor for *Tastemakers*, the school's music magazine, and has been published in *Spectrum*, Northeastern's literary journal. When he graduates, Tim hopes to join the Peace Corps before pursuing a graduate degree in linguistics.

Mara Donofrio

Mara is a Registered Nurse, seamstress, and avid DIY-er in Boston. Her poetry starts as refrigerator magnets.

Simi Esan

Simi loves travelling, watching dark, dramatic TV shows, and asking questions that lead to difficult conversations.

Christine Evers

Christine is a student at Wheaton College in Massachusetts who is studying history and art history. She has been writing poetry since middle school in an attempt to try to sort out all the jumbled thoughts that end up in her brain. Christine can be reached at evers_christine@wheatoncollege.edu.

Rick Faletto

Rick is his most wise walking through the forest. He practices yoga and meditation and thinks *The Tao of Pooh* is an excellent book. He loves dancing, the art of Alex Grey, rock climbing, and exploring new places. Rick also thinks everyone should try moshing at a Streetlight Manifesto show.

Anapurl Feldman

Anapurl is from Wareham, Massachusetts, one of many small towns lost in the abyss of never-heard-of-it, currently studying writing, literature, and publishing at Emerson College in Boston. She likes writing about people and their strangeness and has had her work featured in *Concrete Magazine* and *Noise Medium*.

Elissa Fertig

Elissa is an undergraduate at Northeastern University in Boston. Her poetry has been published in her university's literary magazine, *Spectrum*, and she was a Gold Key winner in flash fiction for the Scholastic Arts & Writing Awards. Inspirations include Mary Oliver and Dean Young.

Fitz Fitzgerald

Fitz is a biomedical engineering student, but he is also working on a historical fiction novel and a poetry album about his faith in God to give to his mom. "How can someone really know themselves if they never first explore their thoughts? So, take a second, and just listen." He can be contacted via email at fitzgerald.m@husky.neu.edu.

Maura K. Flaherty

Maura is currently a senior at Massachusetts Maritime Academy. Her focus there is a Bachelor's in Science, while a passion for writing resides in her core. She can be contacted via email at maura.flaherty@maritime.edu.

Brittany Frederick

Brittany graduated from Stonehill College with a BA in English in 2016. She was awarded her department's top honor for her prose nonfiction piece "Coming Back to Birmingham." At Stonehill, Brittany studied black literature, prose, poetry, fiction, and nonfiction writing. Now, Brittany is a PhD student in Sociology at Boston University where she studies race and inequality. Follow her on Twitter at @Britt_LF and please send inquiries to brittany.frederick2@gmail.com.

Erica Gilman

Erica is a poet, a student, and a laugher. She enjoys reading Rupi Kaur, Andrea Gibson, and Sarah Kay's poetry. If you want to read more of her writing, you can look at her website at gilmanerica.wixsite.com/website, or on her school's online magazine, *The New Worcester Spy*, under poetry.

Madeline Gilmore

Born and raised in North Carolina, Madeline moved to Brooklyn after graduating from Williams College in 2015, when she was awarded the Hubbard Hutchinson Memorial Fellowship for writing. There, she received a Brooklyn Poets Fellowship. Madeline now lives in Boston, where she is pursuing her MFA at Boston University.

Maddie Gloo

Maddie is a Biology undergraduate student at Smith College. She enjoys writing poetry and short stories when she has the time. She is very grateful to be considered for this collection and would like to thank her Mom for always encouraging her writing instinct. Please contact Maddie at mgloo@smith.edu.

Gabe Goodman

Gabe is a writer living in the American northeast. At the time of this submission, he is 21 years old. He is best known for his musical project, titled "Modern Painters." You can hear their work at modernpainters.bandcamp.com or contact him at ModernPaintersBand@gmail.com.

Kiana Govoni

Kiana is currently a university student. She has previously taken fiction and poetry workshops in addition to various courses in literature and writing. One of her earlier poems was published in an award-winning student journal, *The Bridge*.

T.B. Grant

T.B., also known as Grant Tyler Bellino, writes whenever he possibly can. Be it on a napkin, binder from school, or even his arm, he expresses his thoughts through the wonderful world of words.

Henry P. Gray

Henry is a writer, poet, and above all a ships officer. Working offshore and living in Cape Cod, he finds time to write when he can and is in the process of writing a book on the dangers of ships weather routing.

Ben Greenman
Ben is a PhD student studying programming languages at Northeastern University.

Caleigh Grogan
Caleigh is perusing an undergraduate degree in religion at Wheaton College in Norton. Besides reading and writing, Caleigh enjoys dinosaurs, the X-Files, and thinking about owning a dog someday. Caleigh hopes all of these things somehow come in handy in her future of ministry and poetry writing.

Deanna Haas
Deanna is a Boston-based publicist, and when she has it her way, avid writer. A lover of words since childhood, Deanna is a graduate of Bridgewater State University's writing program. When not browsing social media, she can be found reading books or belting Broadway tunes. Follow her on Twitter @deannarhaas.

H.B. Harris
Hamed is a resident of Saugus, Massachusetts. He graduated from Massachusetts Maritime Academy with a degree in engineering and currently works as a consultant for a firm in Boston. He's in active reader and writer, and prefers reading works of fiction, such as Chekhov and Carlos Zafon.

Hadley Heinrich
Hadley is a recent college graduate who has been writing from an early age. She attended Denver School of the Arts in Colorado and has contributed to literary magazines in high school and college. She currently lives in Boston.

James Holbert
James graduated from Bridgewater State University in 2015 where he earned his BA in English Literature. Some of his fiction has appeared in *Driftwood Press*, *Sliver of Stone Magazine*, and *The Bridge*. You can find more of his fiction plus articles on his website at jamesholbert.com.

Paul Horte
In his free time, Paul spends his time as a video game enthusiast, a beer connoisseur, and spends time at indoor rock climbing gyms. Paul also enjoys hiking, movies of all genres, and reading. For further inquiries about writing, please email him at paulhorte@gmail.com.

Jessica Imbro

Jessica is current senior at Northeastern University with a combined major of English and communication studies. She loves eating and her friends and family but not eating her friends and family. She lives in Boston.

Madeleine Jackman

Madeleine was born in California and attended school at the University of Massachusetts, Amherst where she completed an honors poetry project her senior year. She can be reached at madgjackman@gmail.com.

Natalya Jean

Natalya is a queer poet, photographer, and designer living in Boston. She is passionate about spoken word, art, educational issues, and dogs.

Anna Johnson

Anna is a student of comparative literature at Brown University. She enjoys reading and writing poetry, and she finds inspiration for her work in her relationships with friends, family, partners, and strangers on the street about whom she unabashedly speculates. She can be reached at anna.l.c.johnson@gmail.com.

Jordana Joy

Jordana is an aspiring journalist and recent cum laude graduate of Wheaton College, earning a Bachelor's in English. During her time at Wheaton, Jordana was Editor-in-Chief of the student-run newspaper and was published in the *Rushlight* and *Babe Lincoln* literary magazines on campus. Having recently moved to Cleveland, she will be starting an internship with *Ohio Magazine* in January, while working on her first novel. She can best be contacted via email at joy_jordana@wheatoncollege.edu.

Charlotte Koch

Charlotte is a sociology major at the University of Massachusetts, Lowell. She likes cats and spiral staircases. She hopes to be a real person someday soon.

Anika Krause

Anika is a recent graduate of Northeastern University with a degree in English literature. When she's not in the classroom teaching, she loves to read, write, and breathe poetry. You can reach her at krause.an@husky.neu.edu.

Krish Kulka

Krish is a former United States Marine that uses writing as an outlet from his everyday life. An accountant by trade, he finds solace reading in his spare time, trying to read a different genre at least once a month.

Roxxanna Kurtz

Roxxanna is currently a graduate student at Fitchburg State University pursuing her Master's in School Guidance Counseling. When she is not working with children in a daycare, she spends her time writing, drawing, or hanging out with her two cats. Her life motto is "Just keep swimming."

Iris Lapaix

Iris is an Afro-Dominican American born in Boston. She graduated Bridgewater State University with a Bachelor's of Art in History and concentrated in Latin American & Caribbean studies. She is an Assistant Community Coordinator at MassArt's Center for Art and Community Partnership to ignite art and design in neighborhoods.

Chris Lindahl

Chris is a journalist and writer from Massachusetts. He enjoys finding poetry, novelty, and humor in the everyday.

Eloise Lindblom

Eloise is an undergraduate student studying English Literature at Smith College in Northampton, Massachusetts.

K. Dawn Liu

K. Dawn is a student at Smith College in Massachusetts. Her poetry has appeared in *Straight Forward Poetry* and *Labrys Magazine*. When not writing, she enjoys climbing mountains and riding the unicycle. You can find and connect with her at www.kliuarts.com.

Shalen Lowell

Shalen is a transgender and genderfluid writer, blogger, and poet from Boston. They specialize in fiction that represents the intersection of fantasy and postmodern genres and queer literature. Shalen earned their B.A. in English Literature from Stonehill College. Their work has been featured in *Æther & Ichor*, *The Writing Disorder*, and most recently in an edited collection entitled *Privilege Through the Looking Glass*. Shalen can be contacted at shalenlowell@gmail.com.

Callie Ann Marsalisi

Callie is a linguistics student at Northeastern University, about to head off into The Great Unknown (graduate school). In addition to poetry, she also writes both short and long fiction and has completed one stage play that she thinks is funny. Her blog is ColorlessGreenSite.wordpress.com.

Cody Marx

Cody is a college senior pursuing his Bachelor's degree in English and Secondary Education at Bridgewater State University. He writes in East Bridgewater, Massachusetts, and on Twitter @CodyMMarx. This is his second poem.

M. P. Mason

Melissa is a recent graduate from the University of Massachusetts, Amherst. She graduated with a degree in English and a creative writing specialization which she intends to use to become a novelist. In her spare time, Melissa likes to hike, draw, and read (of course).

Meg Maziarz

Meg is from the town of Adams, Massachusetts. She is an avid animal lover and reality TV junkie (regrettably) and stumbled upon a love for writing during her final semesters at Massachusetts College of Liberal Arts in 2014.

Mia Mazzaferro

Mia used to live in the Pioneer Valley, write poetry, and experience joy. Now, she's in nursing school. She has a B.A. from Mount Holyoke College and is now pursuing nurse-midwifery in Boston. She lives with her best friend and a cat named Camp Counselor.

Emily Rosello Mercurio

Emily is currently pursuing her MFA in Creative Writing at Cornell University, where she also teaches composition and has served as Assistant Editor for *EPOCH Magazine*. Her work has appeared in *The Poet's Billow*, *Really System*, and *Plain China*. She is a 2017 winner of the Bermuda Triangle Prize.

Katrina Meserve

Katrina is from the coast of Maine and thinks tattoos are underrated.

Aidan Meyer-Golden
Aidan is an artist from Boston. He makes music under the name Katsu (fredericksun.bandcamp.com). He is a student of mathematics, philosophy, and various languages. Most important to him is his love of Buddha. These various endeavors, though parallel to one another, intersect in his poetry. Feel free to reach out to him about any of these things at afm1212@gmail.com.

Alessandra Miranda
Alessandra is currently a sophomore at Williams College pursuing a Bachelor's of Arts in Statistics. She has been writing and editing poetry since the age of 14. You can reach her at alessandramiranda1013@gmail.com.

Christina Mondy
Christina is a 25-year-old New England native who loves to write. Ironically, she works as a publicist for documentary films. In her free time, she fosters underage kittens, performs improv comedy, and peruses discount racks at grocery stores.

Jennifer Morgan
Jennifer was born and raised in Dallas, Texas, where she learned how to dance badly and make enchiladas. Now she lives with her cat named Bayou and continues to trip frequently and cook stuff.

Eleonora Mortillaro
Ellie is a 23-year-old Bostonian currently living in Florida to get away from the snow. Her writing is majorly inspired by the peacefulness she finds from the natural world. She loves hiking, though she spends most of her time in the waters of the sunny sunshine state.

Keelan P. Murphy
Keelan has had several of his poems and short stories published in his academy's literary magazine and is still uncertain as to how or why. His passion for people and the natural world is often what fuels his work which can be found at www.maritime.edu/turning-tides.

Ty Muto
Ty is a haiku aficionado and cookie monster.

N.F.H.M.

Natalia F. H. Mirabito, a Boston native and self-proclaimed 'decades and antiques nostalgic,' cultivated a passion for writing from an early age. Much of her written poetry reflects a musicality; effortlessly embodied from two decades of classical and contemporary musicianship paired with fine art creations. Her poetry is reminiscent of the nostalgic, as reflected in her syntax and line arrangements of specific words themselves. Natalia completes her undergraduate studies this year, specializing in professional writing and media while exploring professional opportunities in marketing, public affairs, and corporate communications. Within these targeted professional disciplines, she continues to share her love for composing meaningful and passionate works of writing through analytical, academic, and journalistic writing styles.

Katherine Nazzaro

Katherine is a recent graduate from Bridgewater State University. She has been published several times in her school's literary magazine, *The Bridge*, and is currently applying of an MFA in poetry. Updates on her work can be found at katherinenzrr.tumblr.com.

Madeleine Olson

Madeleine is a student at Mount Holyoke College where she pursues a self-designed major concerning artistic expression and engagement. Most recently, she has been recognized with Honorable Mentions from Scholastic Art and Writing Awards (2016) and UCONN Student Writer's Magazine (2016). Olson currently lives in West Hartford, Connecticut.

Ellen Orell

Growing up with Asperger's Syndrome, a high-functioning form of Autism, Ellen was often frustrated with self-expression. She began writing poetry in order to communicate and understand emotions. Her poetry has appeared in a variety of scholastic publications. Besides writing poetry, Orell's passions include teaching, painting, and reading.

Anisha Pai

Anisha is a Mount Holyoke student majoring in computer science and recently won the Glasscock Poetry Prize (2017). Follow @anishapai on Instagram!

Samantha Parker

Ms. Parker is a cadet at the Massachusetts Maritime Academy studying emergency management.

Samuel Henry Penney

Samuel is a third-year mechanical engineering student at Northeastern University in Boston whose poetry and photography have been featured in award-winning literary arts magazines, including Loyola High School's *Windowpanes* and Northeastern's *Spectrum Magazine*. Originally from Pasadena, Sam is honored to be included in this publication.

Natalia Perkins

Natalia is an economics and English double major at Smith College. She mainly enjoys writing poetry based on her past experiences and reflections. She is president of the Smith Ukuleles and sometimes writes her own songs. She hopes to continue writing after college and work in the publishing field.

Jake Phillips

Jake graduated from UMass Amherst in 2017. In his undergraduate career, he was published twice in UMass' literary magazine, *Jabberwocky*. He currently resides in Bridgeport, Connecticut, and plans to enroll in an MFA program next year. Inquiries can be sent to jephillips37@gmail.com.

Julia V. Pretsfelder

Born and raised in New York City, Julia is currently a senior at Amherst College where she majors in English and Latin American studies. She started off writing poetry and is now lost somewhere in her thesis between short stories, rambles, and memoir. She also loves running and photography. You can find some of her work at juliapretsfelder.tumblr.com.

Ashley Puddester

Ashley is proud to be approaching her 20th New England winter. She makes various endeavors to exist. Check out her barren Facebook, Twitter, and Instagram at @cashley080497, for one day these deserts may bloom.

Victoria Pulvidente

Victoria is a writer and poet who recently graduated from Endicott College with a major in English creative writing. She was Editor in Chief of the *Endicott Review* and she currently writes for the Odyssey. You can contact her through   victoriapulvidente@gmail.com   or www.theodysseyonline.com/@victoriapulvidente.

Allister Quilon

Allister is a Boston-based writer who has toured and taught workshops for songwriting and poetry throughout the U.S. and internationally. He is the frontman of the band THE SUNSET KINGS, and will be releasing the group's debut album in the Fall of 2017. Find more work at www.THEsunsetkings.com, or on Instagram and Twitter: @thesunsetkings.

Chris Rinier

Growing up on the water in Southern New England, Christopher is an avid fly-fisherman. He spends his free time tying flies, camping, hiking, and loves connecting with nature. On any giving day, you can find him exploring outside or working on tugboats in Narragansett Bay.

Ashley Robinson

Ashley is a Boston-based writer with an interdisciplinary background in English, graphic design, and dance. Contact Ashley at arobinson.designs@gmail.com.

James Robotham

James studies English literature at UMass Amherst, class of 2018. He plans to pursue a PhD in Literature upon completion of his B.A., and hopes to have enough time to write plenty of poetry in the future.

Randy Rowe

Randy is a graduate of the Massachusetts Maritime Academy, where he pursued a Bachelor's in Emergency Management. He was first exposed to writing serious poetry in a poetry elective while attending school. As a musician, music became one of the main inspirations for the subjects of these poems, including traditional world music from places like Norway and Tuva. It was at this point that Randy learned the power of writing poetry and a new respect for the art grew there afterwards.

Domenic Scopa
Domenic is a four-time Pushcart Prize nominee and the 2014 recipient of the Robert K. Johnson Poetry Prize and Garvin Tate Merit Scholarship. He holds an MFA from Vermont College of Fine Arts. His poetry and translations have been featured in *The Adirondack Review*, *Reed Magazine*, *Borderlands: Texas Poetry Review*, *Reunion: The Dallas Review*, *Belleville Park Pages*, and many others. He is currently a Lecturer at Plymouth State University and a Writing Center Specialist at New Hampshire Technical Institute. His first book, *The Apathy of Clouds* (FutureCycle Press), is forthcoming in 2018. He currently reads manuscripts for Hunger Mountain and is an Associate Editor at Ink Brush Publications.

Dana Shahar
Dana is a multilingual, Singapore-born, Israeli-Canadian-American. She has been writing poetry since the age of 5. On any given day, you can find Dana cooking, gardening, or curled up with her dog and a book. She is majoring in elementary education with sights set on becoming a kindergarten teacher.

Christina Smith
Christina majors in film and new media studies and creative writing and literature at Wheaton College in Norton, Massachusetts. When she's not writing poetry and screenplays, she enjoys tap dancing, petting cats, and watching Coen Brothers movies. She has been published in *Rushlight Literary Magazine*.

Folasade Smith
Folasade is a graduating senior at UMass Dartmouth, majoring in English, writing, rhetoric, and communications. As an aspiring investigative journalist, she has worked with the on-campus newspaper, *The Torch*, as a writer, news editor, and managing editor. She hopes to jump-start her career in Philly as a writer, taking on new and upcoming challenges.

Marina Starkey
Marina received her Bachelor's in Writing, Literature, and Publishing from Emerson College and her Master's from Boston University. Originally from Long Island, she still can't believe she hasn't left Boston yet. When she's not trying to write, you can find her cooking and teaching yoga, hardly ever at the same time.

Alec Suthy

Alec is a visual artist and storyteller based out of Boston. His poems are inspired by surreal art. He can be found on social media under the handle @dilettantishly.

Shem Elias Tane

Shem enjoys short walks on the beach and gumshoes with quick mouths. He will have a new album coming out by his band Watermelon Renaissance. You will be able to find it on Bandcamp and Spotify.

Melinda Cynthia Victoria Taylor

Melinda is a mom, Christian, church member, friend, lover, musician, writer, psychology graduate, childcare provider, ESL tutor, sister, daughter, niece, cousin, and woman with a physical illness who is still trying to figure out life.

Mick Theebs

Mick is a writer of poetry, fiction, and screenplays. He runs the art website ALSO THAT and currently serves as the Poet Laureate of Milford, Connecticut.

Wylie Thornquist

Wylie is a sophomore at Williams College in northwestern Massachusetts, where he studies studio art, art history, and Latin studies. He spends most of his free time drawing, running, spacing out, and thinking about future projects.

Jake Tringali

Jack has lived up and down the East Coast, and then up and down the West Coast, and he is now back in his home city of Boston. Jake runs rad restaurants and thrives in a habitat of bars, punk rock shows, and a sprinkling of burlesque performers. He was first published in 2014. Journals include *Catch & Release, Boston Poetry Magazine, Indiana Voice Journal*, and thirty-five other fine periodicals. Now go enjoy your day. Rock on.

Kayleigh Turgeon

Kayleigh is graduate from University of Massachusetts, Lowell who studied modern languages and creative writing. After graduating, she attended the Salem State Poetry Seminar. Today she works as a high school Spanish teacher and works on her poetry in her free time. She loves traveling, observing nature, reading, and cooking, eating and experiencing foods from many different cultures.

Smith E. Umland
Smith was born and raised in southeastern Connecticut until they began attending Wheaton College in Norton, Massachusetts, where they received a BA in Anthropology. They have been writing poetry since they were very young and have had poems featured in both of Wheaton's literary magazines (*Rushlight* and *Babe Lincoln*). You can find them on Twitter and Instagram @the_bone_queen and more of their poetry at thebonequeen.wordpress.com.

Cole David Vick
Cole is a student in Boston. He's originally from Texas.

Amy Welch
Amy is a young, passionate artist of many interests and talents. During adolescence, at age 14, she self-published a novel and since has discovered a love of poetry and songwriting. Studying to be an actor currently, she is also working on developing herself as a playwright and librettist.

Mikayla Gordon Wexler
Mikayla is a current junior and anthropology major at Amherst College. She hopes to attend medical school and work on urban health policy after she graduates. Mikayla is a die-hard New Englander, and you can usually find her skiing, hiking, or curled up reading by the fire.

April Wildes
April originates from West Allis, Wisconsin, and moved to Boston in 2016 to pursue her MFA at Emerson College.

Greta Wilensky
Greta is a writer from Lowell, Massachusetts. Her fiction and poetry has been published in *Winter Tangerine Review*, *Duende*, *The James Franco Review*, *Souvenir*, *Blueshift Journal*, and elsewhere. She studies writing at Pratt Institute and lives in Brooklyn.

Traci "Troi Justice" Williams
Traci "Troi Justice" is an Ada Comstock Scholar (nontraditional undergraduate student) at Smith College in Northampton. She is a poet, creative writer, and playwright who is majoring in Africana studies and completing a poetry concentration. Williams is married with three children and six grandchildren. Her hometown is Baltimore.

Lizz Wilson

Lizz is a freelance writer, poet, farmer, and self-proclaimed foodie. As a confused millennial, she is trying to balance work and play to achieve satisfaction living a truly creative life.

JinJin Xu

A Shanghai native, JinJin has always lived in between languages and places. Her poetry and nonfiction essays have been published in *Cha*, *The Common Online*, and *Nasty Women Poets: An Anthology of Subversive Verse*. A recent graduate of Amherst College, she is currently traveling the world collecting the voices of dislocated mothers on a Thomas J. Watson fellowship.

Donari Yahzid

Donari is an anthropology and politics double major ready to explore the world.

Chris York

Chris is an attorney in Boston.

H.M Zahra

H.M. is a student of English in Boston and has been writing fiction, poetry, and screenplays since his early teenage years. Having been born in Morocco, it was through literature that he cemented his ability to communicate and connect in a foreign tongue.

Wesline Zolfonoon

Wesline is a fiction writer from Boston and is currently pursuing her MFA in Creative Writing at Emerson College. Her work has been included in *Route 2* literary journal and *Luna Luna*.

73433570R00099

Made in the USA
Lexington, KY
09 December 2017